STEVENAGE AT WAR 1939–1945

John Amess

Published by Stevenage Museum, St. George's Way
Stevenage, Herts. SG1 1XX

ISBN 0948754 11 7

Front cover design by Stevenage Museum
Printed by Crompton Press Ltd. Letchworth

Front Cover Illustration:
Bren gun carriers belonging to the regular army assisting the Home Guard to clear the town of 'enemy' forces. The photograph was taken during the invasion exercise held in 1942 and shows the front of the Methodist Church looking towards the junction of Sish Lane with the High Street. (The Pictorial)

CONTENTS

FOREWORD .... (iii)

ACKNOWLEDGMENTS .... (iv)

INTRODUCTION .... (v)

Chapter 1 STEVENAGE WAR REPORTS: JULY 1935 TO DECEMBER 1944 ... 1

Chapter 2 THE LAST FEW MONTHS: JANUARY TO MAY 1945 59

Chapter 3 "I SHALL ALWAYS REMEMBER............" 65

LIST OF ABBREVIATIONS 73

BIBLIOGRAPHY 75

FOREWORD

The author and his associates are to be congratulated on an excellent job in putting together a chronicle of local wartime events, which should be of considerable interest to the people of Old Stevenage, and I would hope to the new residents of the town too.

The book will revive many old memories not least of friendships formed by service during the war. It is a useful and worthy book to set beside those recording events in Stevenage since that period.

Philip T. Ireton

As a member of the pre-war Urban District Council, Mr. Ireton was given a major role in formulating the Air Raid Precaution plans for Stevenage. He was later appointed Officer-in-Charge of the town A.R.P. Report and Control Centre, and served in that capacity throughout the early war years.

INTRODUCTION

People who are asked to recall their memories of civilian life during the Second World War, will often recount amusing incidents and talk of comradeship. In reality, the war also brought considerable anxiety and hardship. The frequent air raids, the threat of invasion, the shortage of food and other essentials, plus numerous wartime restrictions, all imposed a great strain on the population. For many, the war also brought destruction and grief, as towns and cities were bombed and thousands of people killed or injured. Looking back, it is chilling to realise just how near Britain came to being enslaved by an inhuman regime. The fact that the nation survived the onslaught and remained free, owes much to the courage and endurance of the civilian population.

"Stevenage at War: 1939-45", illustrates the effect of the war on a small country town 31 miles north of London. In the 1930's, Stevenage had a population of less than 6000 and was spread over approximately 4500 acres. Although small, the town was involved in all the major Home Front activities of the Second World War. During 1937/38 the Urban District Council organised volunteer emergency services to deal with wartime fires, poison gas contamination, and casualties. By the time the war began in September 1939, several hundred children and adults had been evacuated to homes in the town. Although some distance from London, Stevenage also experienced many fringe effects of the 1940/41 Blitz. Londoners who lost their homes during the Blitz came to Stevenage seeking temporary accommodation; others came to spend a night away from the bombing. Local Auxiliary Fire Service units volunteered to serve in London and were in action fighting some of the worst fires in history. Although bomb damage in Stevenage was slight, several enemy aircraft, probably lost, ditched their bomb load in the surrounding area. The town also provided canteen facilities, accommodation and welfare services for the personnel of military convoys using the Great North Road.

Chapter 1, which forms the bulk of the record, chronicles Stevenage wartime activities from July 1935 to the end of 1944, in the form of brief monthly reports. The reports are structured as if written at the time and make use of information gathered from a variety of sources, including interviews with former members of local emergency service units. Reports of events and activities which occurred frequently throughout the war years have been limited to typical examples only. Whilst just a few of the people directly involved in Stevenage wartime activites are mentioned by name, it will become obvious to the reader that there were many many more whose service will probably never be recorded. The Stevenage Society for Local History or Stevenage Museum would be pleased to receive suggestions for additions to the record.

ACKNOWLEDGEMENTS

I am indebted to the staff of the following organisations for their help in my search for information: Stevenage Museum, Stevenage Central Library, Hitchin Museum, Stevenage Borough Council, Herts. County Record Office and the North Herts. Gazette Group.

My grateful thanks are also due to the townsfolk listed below, who so generously allowed me to probe their memories of wartime Stevenage. Without their contribution, this record would have been very sparse:-

Mr. I. Batley
Mrs. A. Batley
Mr. C. Bentley
Mrs. B. Bentley
Mr. G. Briars
Mrs. M. Briars
Mr. J. Briars
Mrs. M. Briars
Mr. S. Chalkley
Mrs. F. Chalkley
Mr. F. Chance
Mrs. F. Chance
Mr. A. Cotts
Mrs. I. Cotts
Mrs. E. Davis
Mr. C. Fairey
Miss M. Farris
Mr. R. Freeman
Mr. R.T. Garner
Mr. W. Gathercole
Mrs. D. Griffith
Mrs. D. Guest
Mr. A.G. Halling
Mrs. L. Halling
Mr. C. Hawkins
Mrs. G. Hawkins
Mr. A. Horsfield
Mrs. E. Horsfield
Miss B. Howard
Miss M. Howard
Mrs. D. Hunt
Mr. P. Ireton
Mrs. W. Ivory
Mr. A. Lines
Mr. E. Moore
Mr. C. Newberry
Mrs. M. Newberry
Miss N. Norman
Mrs. Norman
Mrs. D. Richardson
Mrs. F. Routledge
Mr. K. Sell
Mr. J. Shepherd
Mr. D. Sidley
Mr. A. Toll
Mr. G. Usher
Mr. W. Ward
Mrs. J. Ward
Mr. R. Warren
Mrs. E. Watson
Mr. T. Welch
Mrs. C. Welch
Mr. R. Welch
Mrs. K. Welch

The photographs which were originally published in 'The Pictorial', have been included by kind permission of the 'The Comet'. Whilst I have indicated, where known, the source of the other photographs, I have been unsuccessful in tracing all the copyright owners and apologize to those I have missed. The extracts from the Letchmore Road School log-book, have been included by kind permission of the Headmistress, Mrs. M.G. Atkinson.

Finally, my grateful thanks to the members of The Stevenage Society for Local History, for their help and encouragement. I am particularly indebted to Paul Tuffery, Anne Grimshaw and Roy Findley. To Paul for reading the original draft and his many suggestions for improving the text, and to Anne for proof reading the final draft. Roy comes from an old Stevenage family and as a teenager served as a member of the town A.R.P. Services. Roy introduced me to most of the folk I interviewed and also provided invaluable information on wartime Stevenage.

Civil Defence observers standing in the grounds of Holy Trinity Church during the invasion exercise held in 1942. (The Pictorial)

Chapter 1

STEVENAGE WAR REPORTS: JULY 1935 TO DECEMBER 1944

During the First World War the enemy successfully used aircraft to attack Britian, and bombed civilian as well as military targets. The post war defence planning authorities recognised that such raids would almost certainly be a feature of any future European war, and that pre-arranged schemes for the protection of the civilian population would be essential. Initially, civil defence plans were prepared by the Committee of Imperial Defence, but in 1935 this responsibility passed to the newly established Air Raid Precautions (A.R.P) Department of the Home Office. In July 1935, the Home Office requested all local government authorities to prepare civil defence schemes in accordance with a series of Circulars to be published by the A.R.P. Department. The schemes were to include: giving A.R.P. instructions to the public; means of giving air raid warnings; recruitment and training of A.R.P. workers; provision of rescue and first aid services; distribution of gas masks; gas detection and cleansing; provision of public air raid shelters; protection of A.R.P. premises; control of public lighting; and co-ordination of A.R.P. services. The reports begin in 1935 when the first Home Office Circular was received by the Stevenage Urban District Council.

JULY, 1935

The following item was entered into the minutes of the Stevenage Urban District Council General Purposes Committee meeting, held on Friday 9th July, 1935:-

"AIR RAID PRECAUTIONS. Copies of a Circular dated 9th instant, on the precautions to be taken in the event of air attacks, were received from the Home Office, in which it was stated that the arrangements to be made by local authorities in connection with each service, would be described in a series of memorandum to be issued by the Air Raid Precautions Department of the Home Office."

NOVEMBER, 1935

For administration purposes, the Herts. County Council Air Raid Precautions Committee, divided the county into nine local A.R.P. areas. Hitchin, Baldock, Letchworth, Royston and Stevenage comprise area no. 4.

OCTOBER, 1936

The Stevenage Urban District Council (referred to simply as the Council from this point on), are to form an Air Raid Precautions Committee.

JANUARY, 1937

The Air Raid Precautions Act which came into force on January 1st, imposes on local authorities the duty to prepare general A.R.P. schemes.

MARCH, 1937

The Government announced plans to form an Air Raid Wardens Service, and the Home Secretary has broadcast an appeal for more volunteer A.R.P. workers.

APRIL, 1937

Following successful completion of an anti-gas training course held in the town, approximately 60 Stevenage residents offer their services to the Council.

JUNE, 1937

Following a directive issued by the Home Office, the Council are calling for volunteers to form a Stevenage Auxiliary Fire Service (A.F.S), which is to reinforce the existing town volunteer fire brigade. Posters displayed in the town call on men aged between 25 and 50 to volunteer, and state that former members of the town volunteer fire brigade will be particularly welcome. The Council are offering a bonus of £1 to every man who completes the necessary training. Mr. Bosley, a town coal merchant, has been engaged to provide vehicles and to give driving instruction at a cost of 3/- per hour. The Council bought twelve electrically non-conducting helmets from Messrs. Merryweather & Son, at a cost of £1-7-6 each. The new A.F.S. volunteers and the town brigade are to train together and share the Fire Station in Basil's Road. Initially, 12 volunteers are required for the A.F.S. but this number is expected to increase to include telephonists and associated units in surrounding villages. The volunteers will be examined by the town Medical Officer of Health, at a fee of 5/- each.

MARCH, 1938

The Home Secretary broadcast an appeal for one million A.R.P. volunteers, following Hitler's seizure of Austria.

JULY, 1938

At a meeting of the Council A.R.P. Committee, it was estimated that 172 volunteers would be required to meet the needs of the Stevenage A.R.P. Services. Since the existing number of volunteers falls well short of this figure, the Council decided to open a recruiting office at 26 High Street.

SEPTEMBER, 1938

In order to encourage recruits, the Council placed the following advertisement in local newspapers:-

STEVENAGE URBAN DISTRICT COUNCIL.
VOLUNTEERS URGENTLY WANTED FOR A.R.P. SCHEMES
You may enrol for any of the undermentioned services:
AUXILIARY FIRE SERVICE, AIR RAID WARDENS, FIRST AID,
RESCUE, DECONTAMINATION, AMBULANCE DRIVERS,
CLERICAL ASSISTANTS, MESSENGERS, STOREKEEPERS, etc.

Please apply at:-

COUNCIL OFFICES to 5.30 p.m. - Sat. to 1.00 p.m.
or
26 HIGH STREET 6-8.00 p.m.

The Air Raid Warden Service is to provide the most direct link between the general public and the authorities. For organisational purposes, the town has been divided into two sections. West of the High Street has been designated Section 'A' and east of the High Street, Section 'B'. Each Section is to be under the control of a Head Warden and sub-divided into 5 Sectors. Sectors A1 to A5, and B1 to B5. Each Sector will be the responsibility of a Senior Warden, a Deputy Warden, and (on average) four Wardens. This structure will give the requirement of an average of one Warden for every 100 inhabitants.

Each Warden will be expected to have a thorough knowledge of his or her Sector, ie. its inhabitants, the buildings, the location of services such as gas, electricity and water, and the availability of public shelters, etc. They are to advise inhabitants of the recommended air raid precautions, request and assist the emergency services in the event of an incident in their Sector, and give immediate aid where possible. They will also be required to help with the distribution and maintenance of gas masks. There are to be fifteen designated Wardens Posts in Stevenage. It is expected that the homes of some Sector Wardens will be used as Posts. Such homes will be protected against bomb blast and linked by telephone to the Report and Control Centre. Later, two purpose built Wardens Posts are to be constructed.

The Council have bought a siren for £12 from Messrs. Robert Maclean & Co. Ltd. (to use as an air raid warning siren), and also granted approval for a further course of first aid and A.R.P. lectures to be given at the Town Hall. The cost of the course is to be met by the Herts. County Council but the trainees will be expected to buy their own textbooks. Other items bought by the Council at this time include 80 copies of the A.R.P. Handbook No.8. "The Duties of Air Raid Wardens". The total Council expenditure on A.R.P. activities at this time amounted to £374, of which the Government is expected to pay 65%.

Gas masks kits were delivered to the town about the middle of the month, and were assembled the same day by dozens of townsfolk. The following day over 5000 completed masks were distributed throughout the town. Anti-gas training sessions are being held each evening at the Town Hall for 105 A.R.P. workers, but the Council is still appealing for further volunteers who could serve as Air Raid Wardens during the day. Air raid shelter trenches have been dug at Bury Mead, the Grammar School playing field, and on the Green by Letchmore Road School.

OCTOBER, 1938

A First Aid Post has been established in the town Welfare Centre at 27 High Street, for the treatment of casualties suffering from minor injuries and/or those contaminated with mustard gas. Persons seriously injured and/or contaminated with phosgene or chlorine, will be treated in a local emergency hospital.

A hut at the rear of the Club and Institute at 31 High Street, is being adapted to serve as a depot for the town A.R.P. Ambulance Service and First Aid Parties. Ambulances (or vehicles converted to ambulances), are to be used to transport casualties from the site of an incident, to the First Aid Post or hospital. An ambulance crew will generally comprise a driver and assistant, plus two attendants with some knowledge of first aid and anti-gas treatment. The First Aid Parties are to be trained and equipped to give first aid treatment at the site of an incident. The A.R.P. Ambulance Service will also include several owner-drivers, who will use their own cars as 'sitting case' ambulances.

The Council premises in Church Lane (the town maintenance yard), is to be used as a depot for the Rescue Squad and Decontamination Squad. The Rescue Squad will be trained to rescue casualties trapped in bomb damaged buildings, and also to demolish dangerous structures and clear away debris. Rescue Squad workers will generally be recruited from the building trades and therefore accustomed to handling the equipment required. The Decontamination Squad will be trained to remove all traces of dangerous and persistent gas from streets, vehicles and buildings. Since it will be necessary for the Decontamination Squad to operate in very heavy protective clothing, the men recruited to this service will need to be physically fit and accustomed to heavy manual labour. The Council Engineer will control the two services with a foreman in charge of each.

Arrangements are made for laundries to provide a service for the decontamination of clothing contaminated with poison gas. Clothing from Stevenage is to be sent to the Pioneer Garden City Laundry Limited, Pixmore Avenue, Letchworth, where special equipment has been installed.

NOVEMBER, 1938

The town civil defence service units had the opportunity to put into practice their months of training. A county wide night exercise was arranged during which several realistic incidents were staged, including eight at Stevenage. One incident involved the rescue of a person trapped under a collapsed roof on the top storey of the training structure at Broomin Green; in another, the High Street Post Office was supposed to have received several direct hits from incendiary bombs. Perhaps the most bizarre incident was the rescue of a 'casualty' thrown by blast into a large water filled cistern in Scoot's Yard, Walkern Road. Very Lights were dropped from aircraft, and one was reported to have fallen on the E.S.A. factory. Gas masks were worn by participants during some of the incidents. All the town A.R.P. Services were involved including local Boy Scouts serving as messengers and dummy casualties. Although some of the incidents were omitted due to lack of time, all the workers had a busy night. A team of ladies served refreshments at the Town Hall when the exercise was over.

The Stevenage A.R.P. Committee are meeting at least once a week to deal with the increase in civil defence activities.

Townsfolk were given an opportunity to test their gas masks at the "L.N.E.R.,A.R.P. Instruction Unit", which was parked at Stevenage Station for one week. The Unit was housed in a converted dining car and included a gas chamber.

A.R.P. stores bought by the Council as this time include the following items:-

"1 STAND PIPE, 2.5in., £3.0.0
4 50ft LENGTHS OF HOSE, 2.25in., £16–13–4
2 JET SPRAY NOZZLES (decontamination of roads), £9–2–0
6 GALVANIZED BINS (bleaching protective clothing), £12-0-0
12 DUST BLINDS (for the First Aid Post), £3–12–0

A public demonstration of incendiary bomb fire fightingtechniques,werepresented at the E.S.A. Sports Ground, when a practice bomb was ignited on the roof of a dummy house. The upper storey of the two storey structure was furnished as a bedroom and covered with a corrugated iron roof. The bomb quickly burnt through the corrugated iron and fell into the bedroom, setting it on fire. Within two minutes, the bomb burnt through the bedroom floor and fell onto the ground below. A 'stirrup' pump, (a hand operated water pump used by the A.R.P. Services), plus approximately six gallons of water were needed to extinguish the bedroom fire, but the bomb had to be dealt with by the A.F.S. using their light trailer pump.

JANUARY, 1939

The inaugural meeting of the Stevenage branch of the "A.R.P. Women's Voluntary Services", was held on Thursday 12th January at the home of Mrs. Mott in Fairview Road. Some 30 potential members attended this first meeting and a committee was formed with Mrs. Mott as Chairman and Mrs. E. Horsfield as Secretary. This service was introduced in June 1938 and was initially intended to act solely as a recuiting agency for the A.R.P. Services. It is now intended that the activities of the organisation be extended to encompass many other civil defence and general welfare functions, and that the name of the service be changed to "Women's Voluntary Services for Civil Defence" (W.V.S.)

The first W.V.S. committee meeting, held a week later, discussed the problem of evacuees. It was noted that the Council had protested that Stevenage was not a suitable evacuation area due to its close proximity to London, but that the appeal had failed and the Council were obliged to send a letter to all residents telling of their intention to conduct a billeting census. The Council asked the W.V.S. to help with the census, as indicated by the following extract from the minutes of the committee:-

> "On January 19th a committee meeting was held at the small Town Hall to discuss the billeting census. It was arranged to split this work into two sections, one to commence on January 23rd, the other on January 30th. It was decided to ask the General Meeting for 17 volunteers from each section. Volunteers were also needed for the clerical work which would be entailed when the books were returned.
>
> It was proposed ... that a letter should be sent to the Council requesting that our Chairman, Mrs. Mott, be allowed to attend all committee meetings dealing with the Evacuation Scheme.
>
> It was also proposed ... that the Council be asked for a room and typewriter to be placed at our disposal."

The Council agreed to let members of the W.V.S. Committee attend any meeting at which evacuees are to be discussed, and also provided them with a room in the Council premises at 9 Orchard Road. The rent for the room (which is presumably to be paid out of A.R.P funds), was fixed at 12/6 per week inclusive of heating and lighting.

The proposed Evacuation Scheme is to provide accommodation for groups of school children and their teachers, young children accompanied by their mothers or some other responsible person, expectant mothers, adult blind persons and cripples. Although it is expected that many buildings will be requisitioned as evacuee hostels, it is also recognised that billeting evacuees in private accommodation will also be essential and probably compulsory. To avoid the inevitable chaos that would result from a panic exodus of areas under attack, the scheme aims to evacuate large numbers of people from high to low risk regions before war begins.

The Council authorised the erection of a steel structure at the Fire Station in Basil's Road, to be used for drying fire hoses and also to carry a new fire alarm.

A course of twelve civil defence lectures was given at Alleyne's Grammar School to local A.R.P. workers.

FEBRUARY, 1939

To co-ordinate the A.R.P. Services during an emergency, a Report & Control Centre is being established in two ground floor rooms (one for Report and one for Control), in the Council premises at 9 Orchard Road. There are to be three tables in the Report Room and two in the Control Room, with five telephones linking the Centre to the A.R.P. depots. On the wall adjacent to the 'outward telephone table' is to be a pin board covered with a town map. Messages regarding an incident will be received in the Report room, and then passed to the Control room officer who will direct the appropriate services into action. Stevenage Report and Control Centre will also serve the surrounding villages of Graveley, Aston, Benington, Knebworth, Shephall, Walkern, and Ardeley. Mr. P.T. Ireton has been appointed Officer in Charge of the Centre, and Runners (or Messengers as they are to be called), will be recruited to carry messages in the event of a telephone failure.

MARCH, 1939

A summary of the town billeting census has been sent to the Ministry of Health, stating that the available accommodation in Stevenage is suitable for: 807 unaccompanied children, 94 teachers and helpers, 101 others, and 656 private reservations. (A total of 1658 persons).

Mrs. Montague Norman, the speaker at a recent W.V.S. meeting, spoke of the various tasks which were to be undertaken by the W.V.S., and she made particular reference to the apprehension regarding evacuees. She stressed that the "dumplings" as she called the evacuees, were unlikely to be criminals, verminous, or tubercular as implied by current rumours. The London authorities, she assured her listeners, were unlikely to wish to bring discredit on themselves by allowing such children to be evacuated to private homes. (Whether this meeting calmed or raised any fears held by the townsfolk, is unrecorded. However, there can be little doubt that the people of Stevenage recognise that the transfer of children from one home to another, is unlikely to prove easy).

APRIL, 1939

Letchmore Road School Log-Book entry (abbreviated to simply "Sch. Log" for all future entries):"...A.R.P. Officer visited the school and discussed the nature of trenches to be dug in time of emergency and also the positioning of such trenches".

The W.V.S., in their capacity as a recruiting agency for the A.R.P. Services, have been asked to find volunteers to staff the town First Aid Post. They have responded by forming a local detatchment of the British Red Cross Society. Mrs. S. White has been appointed Commandant, and Dr. B.L. Skeggs the Medical Officer.

A report in the Herts. and Beds. Express dated 22nd, states that the Stevenage A.R.P. Services still require a further 8 Wardens, plus 5 volunteers for First Aid Parties; 3 for the Rescue Party and 4 for the Decontamination Squad. The same issue of the newspaper also carries an appeal for volunteers to join the Territorial Regiments, the Police Specials, the St. John Ambulance Brigade and the Red Cross. In the face of continuing reluctance by the public to believe that war is likely, there seem to be too many organisations chasing too few volunteers. To make matters worse, many local commercial concerns (notably the E.S.A) are forming their own A.R.P. units and calling for volunteers from the workforce. This latter situation has been the cause of several resignations from the Council A.R.P. Services, and the Clerk of the Council has been instructed to protest to the commercial organisations concerned. The authorised strength of A.R.P. Services for Stevenage (based on Home Office recommendations as determined by the Herts. County Council A.R.P. Committee), has been declared as follows:-

A.R.P. WARDENS	52 MEN & 12 WOMEN
FIRST AID PARTIES (3)	15 MEN
FIRST AID POST (1)	4 MEN & 16 WOMEN
AMBULANCE UNIT	20 WOMEN for 5 Ambulances & 3 WOMEN for 3 sitting case cars.
LIGHT RESCUE PARTY	7 MEN
DECONTAMINATION SQUAD	7 MEN
REPORT CENTRE	4 MEN & 6 WOMEN
MESSENGERS	8 MEN

The age regulations are given as: 25 years minimum for Rescue Parties, First Aid Parties and Decontamination Squads; 30 years minimum for Wardens, Ambulance and First Aid Post personnel and 45 years minimum for Report Centre staff. Messengers to be over 40 years of age or under 18.

In addition to the various A.R.P. Services, the Police force is also directly involved in civil defence duties. For example, it is the duty of the Police to take charge and co-ordinate the emergency services at an incident. The strength of the Police force is to be increased by the addition of Police War Reserve, Womens' Auxiliary Police Corps, and Special Constables. Stevenage men who served as Special Constables during the General Strike, have been recalled to serve during this new emergency. The Specials are to work with the town regular Police Force and use the Police Station in Stanmore Road.

A meeting of the Stevenage and District Chamber of Trade, held at Mr. Hutchinson's restaurant 35 High Street, heard a lecture on the protection of buildings.

The ever increasing volume of civil defence activities has prompted the Council to advertise for a part-time paid assistant. From twelve applicants the Council have selected a Mr. Flint to be the Stevenage A.R.P. Officer.

MAY, 1939

The following entry was made in the minutes of the W.V.S. meeting held on May 19th:-

> "Mrs. Margetts then read the Home Office letter dealing with evacuation in which it was stated that the help of the W.V.S. was essential for the efficient working of the scheme. It was also learnt that it would be necessary to provide extra clothing for the children concerned.
>
> Mrs. Martin-Smith's letter was then read concerning the reception of the crippled and blind children and of expectant mothers. It was suggested that Mrs. Margetts approach Mr. Marsden Popple and put the relevant facts before him, stressing the desirability of providing a suitable building for the reception of evacuees.
>
> It was resolved to ask Mr. Greenwood if he could provide St. John Ambulance men to be at the Railway Station on the arrival of the evacuated children and others. It was also decided to enlist the services of Mrs. Lang (midwife) in this connection. It was learnt that the children billeted at Stevenage were to be marched to the E.S.A. and provided with rations. Two billeting assistants to supervise the arrangements for each road."

JUNE, 1939

Although some members of the W.V.S. are to have the chance to relax for a few hours when they attend a civil defence rally in Hyde Park next month, the number of serious tasks being undertaken by the service continues to grow. The following item was entered in the minutes of the W.V.S. meeting held on the 21st June:-

> "NATIONAL SERVICES RALLY, JULY 2ND.
> With regard to this it was learned that 10 W.V.S. representatives were to be sent from Hertfordshire and 10 from Sussex. Stevenage having the honour to be selected. Representatives to meet at Hatfield on June 26th to be fitted for W.V.S. uniforms and to practice marching ... A letter from the Matron of Hitchin Hospital was next read, stating that provision was to made for 57 extra beds, and a stock of garments would therefore be required as listed ... Whist Drives should be arranged to raise funds for Hospital Supplies ..."

JULY, 1939

To strengthen the control of civil defence in war time, particularly if communication with Government authorities becomes difficult or impossible, the country has been divided into twelve independent regions, each under the direction of a Regional Commissioner. The Regional Commissioner is responsible for co-ordination of the civil defence activities within the region, and is empowered to act on behalf of the Government if necessary. Stevenage comes within the Eastern Region, which has its Headquarters in Cambridge. Local government authorities are also required to appoint an A.R.P. Controller and an Emergency Committee to whom they can delegate local civil government in the event of a crisis. The Council have appointed Mr. A. Primett (Clerk of the Council) to act as A.R.P. Controller, and have formed an Emergency Committee comprising Messrs. J.A. Marsden Popple, F.J. Blow and R.H. Walker.

The following stores have been added to the Council collection of A.R.P. equipment:-

26 WARDENS POST REPORT BOOKS
30 METAL STRETCHERS
50 WARDEN BADGES
2 CARTONS OF MEDICAL STORES
10 STRETCHER CARRY PACKS
60 CURTAINS
30 WARDENS PLATES (HOUSE PLATES)
20 PAIRS OF GLOVES, SMALL
2 DRUMS OF BLEACH POWDER
1 STIRRUP PUMP
10 STEEL HELMETS
30 PAIRS GUM-BOOTS, MENS
28 CURTAINS

The annual Hospital Day Parade wound its way along Stevenage High Street on Saturday the 8th, and included features which reminded the townsfolk of the threat of war and of A.R.P. preparations. The lads of Symonds Green, well known for their comic floats, entered a float entitled the SYMONDS GREEN ALLSILLERY FIRE BRIGADE. In addition to a weird collection of fire fighting apparatus, the float carried a notice stating that "Calls would be answered by return of post". The parade also included members of the real Stevenage A.R.P. Services: the A.F.S. complete with two trailer pumps; a contingent of Wardens; the Decontamination Squad dressed in their protective clothing; one of the town fire engines; and a float depicting W.V.S. activities. By way of contrast, the Young People's Fellowship, who believe that the emergency preparations are more likely to cause war than prevent it, entered a float entitled "Peace unto all Nations".

AUGUST, 1939

The A.F.S. cancelled the practice of patrolling the town with their pumps, in favour of keeping them at three strategic locations. One pump is to be kept near the E.S.A. works, one near the Stevenage Motor Company, and the third at Pin Green.

Members of the Stevenage Auxiliary Fire Service team with their fire engine. The photograph was taken in Church Lane looking towards the rear of the fire station.
c1940 (Mr. A. G. Halling)

A.R.P. Stores received this month:-

1 FIREMANS AXE	2 3in. ACETYLENE FLARES
1 CROSS-CUT SAW, 4ft	1 'DUFT NORTON' LIFTING JACK
50 STEEL HELMETS	2 50yrd ROLLS WATERPROOF SHEET
1 LIFTING GEAR, 13cwt	1 PAIR ROPE PULLEY BLOCKS
1 PICK-AXE	50 ANTI-DIM OUTFITS
12 FIRST AID BOXES	24 PADS, MESSENGER FORMS
1 PROTECTIVE HELMET	10 HOODS

3 15ft GALVANIZED STEEL WIRES FOR SCAFFOLD LASHINGS

In parallel with the increase in international tension during the past few months, the pace of civil defence preparations has also increased. Many A.R.P. schemes have come into full effect. To avoid showing lights to raiders, windows of buildings likely to be used after dark have been fitted with temporary 'black-out-screens'. Vehicle lamps have been covered with light reducing masks. Kerbstones, lamp-posts, pillar-boxes, corners of buildings, etc., have been painted white to aid movement after dark. Gas detection boards have been erected at regular intervals throughout the town, and the public has been warned to carry their gas masks at all times. Essential buildings have been protected with sandbags, and the windows of public buildings and shops have been covered with a fabric mesh or tape, to reduce the danger from flying glass splinters caused by bomb blast. Trenches have been dug in the wide grass verge along the north-west side of the High Street, for use by shoppers caught in the open during an air raid. (A sign on a nearby building states: "100 YRDS TO AIR RAID SHELTER"). The town Evacuation Officer has bought 20 yards of white linen, at a cost of 5/–, to make into armbands for the Billeting Officers, and a tribunal has been formed to deal with any evacuation problems. The town A.R.P. Services have been called to full operational state, and the A.R.P. Controller and the Emergency Committee have been granted full executive powers.

SEPTEMBER, 1939

Most of the evacuees directed to Stevenage, arrived at the beginning of the month. 400 unaccompanied children, 27 teachers, and 300 mothers with children arrived during the first two days. (A total of 1600 evacuees are expected). The evacuees were met at the station by the town Evacuation Officer, Chief Receiving Officer, Chief Billeting Officer and some 40 helpers. Each of the evacuees were given tea and biscuits on arrival, plus a small ration of food to take with them to their billets.

Porters from Billingsgate Fish Market outside a warehouse adjacent to Stevenage railway station. During September 1939, when this photograph was taken, the London market was closed and fish distribution centres were established in various parts of the country. One centre came to Stevenage. (The Pictorial)

In a statement broadcast at 11.15 a.m. on Sunday, 3rd September, the Prime Minister told the nation that all efforts to persuade Germany against initiating further hostile actions toward her neighbours had failed, and that consequently Britain has no alternative but to declare war.

Although it is still widely believed that a war on the scale of the First World War is unlikely and that the crisis will probably be over in a few weeks, few people can have received this news without some feeling of anxiety for the future. Air raids are expected to commence at any time and final civil defence preparations are being hurriedly completed. Many wartime regulations have been brought into full effect. The Stevenage Emergency Committee is meeting daily to direct local civil defence activities, and the appointment of the town A.R.P. Officer has been extended to full time. Another full time worker has been appointed to the Report and Control Centre. The Council are to buy a Commer van for £80 from G.E. Harper's Garage, to use as an ambulance, and arrangements have been made for the town A.R.P. Services to obtain petrol supplies from a designated pump at the Stevenage Motor Company.

The annual Stevenage Fair which was due to be held in the High Street on the 22nd and 23rd, was cancelled (although Mrs. Smith did set up her sweet rock stall in the High Street as usual). The Council have turned down a Herts. County Council request to provide additional mortuary facilities. The intention was that Stevenage mortuary should also cater for the surrounding villages. It is the opinion of the Council, that the facilities they have provided will only just be adequate to meet the needs of Stevenage.

A town Food Control Committee has been formed, which includes the following local traders: Mr. C.H. Mott a retail grocer, Mr. H. O'Clee a butcher, Mr. T.E. Beswick of the Co-op, and Mr. C. Jones. The Ministry of Agriculture and Fisheries has urged all local authorities to take possession of any unused land, by requisition if necessary, for use as allotments. A Fuel Control Committee has also been formed.

The tenant of the cottage situated in the Council premises in Church Lane has been rehoused to allow part of the cottage to be converted into a Gas Cleansing Station. The Parish Rooms in Basil's Road have been opened as a Social Centre for evacuated mothers and their children. The Centre is being run by a committee comprising: the Rev. L. Fuller-Higgs (Bunyan Baptist Church), the Rev, K.H. Hart (C of E), the Rev. J. Heaven (Methodist Church), plus two members from each congregation. With the help of the 1st Stevenage Guides, the Centre is providing light refreshment and facilities for letter writing.

The Council have refused permission for the residents of Letchmore Green to dig air raid trenches on their Green. The Council stated that the trenches being dug at this time were intended only for shoppers caught in the open during an air raid.

The residents of the south end of Fairview Road, are worried that the light coloured roofs of Stevenage Laundry and the G.W. King Works expose them to an increased risk of air attack. In reply to their petition, the Council stated that these two roofs as well as similar roofs in the town are due to be camouflaged. (The side of the E.S.A. factory facing the railway has been camouflaged to look like cottages).

From September 29th, everyone is required to carry an Identity Card at all times.

Sch. Log, Sept. 13th, "School opened on a voluntary basis. Number on the books 269, number present 158. Trenches not yet started: this is the reason for the voluntary attendance. Order 'darken' windows given to Messrs. Toll Bros. School hours at present from 9 to 12.45 p.m. ....and gardening are carried on in the afternoon."

Sch. Log, Sept. 18th,"The Heads of the two LCC evacuated schools met here at 10 a.m. to receive stock for their schools which are to be in session this afternoon from 1 to 4.30 p.m. Total collected by the boys on Hospital Saturday, £18.11.0. From today, Monday, school hours are:-

STEVENAGE 9-12.30 L.C.C. 1-4.30

OCTOBER, 1939

Sch. Log, Oct. 9th, "Major General Lucas and the contractors for trench digging called at the school."

Sch. Log, Oct. 10th, "Major General Lucas called and inspected the setting out of the school trenches."

Sch. Log, Oct. 12th, "Permission received from the County Land Agents Office Hertford, for the boys of the school to take over plots numbered 1, 2, 3 and 8 for the duration of the war." (Note: Plots are allotments to be used for growing vegetables).

A room in the Town Hall is being opened on Sundays from 12.30 p.m. to 5.00 p.m., for use by parents visiting their evacuee children. The Grange, No.5 High Street, has been re-opened to house 100 evacuee boys not suitable for normal billeting. The W.V.S. have been asked to help bath the boys and mend their clothes. (The school originally at The Grange, has been moved to Yarlet Hall at Stone in Staffordshire). 1st Stevenage Scout Troop has begun collecting waste paper to be sold in aid of the Red Cross, and a lady living in the High Street has been fined £1 for infringing the 'black-out' regulations.

The fire services have been re-grouped into national regions, which in turn have been sub-divided into Districts. Stevenage comes within District No.7.

Further appeals are being made in local newspapers for ex-soldiers aged 45 and over, to join the National Defence Companies. These units, which are affiliated to the Territorial Army, are to be used to guard important installations such as railway bridges, tunnels, docks, etc.

Although some members of the A.R.P. Services are tending to become bored with the inactivity of the so-called 'phoney war', the work of the W.V.S. is steadily increasing. Fund raising events such as jumble sales and whist drives, are being organised by the W.V.S. to support their various working parties. (The working parties are making garments etc. for supply to the forces and local hospitals). The W.V.S. are also running classes in first aid, home nursing, cooking and elementary A.R.P. precautions. The local branch of the Women's Unionist Association are also active in support of the W.V.S. work.

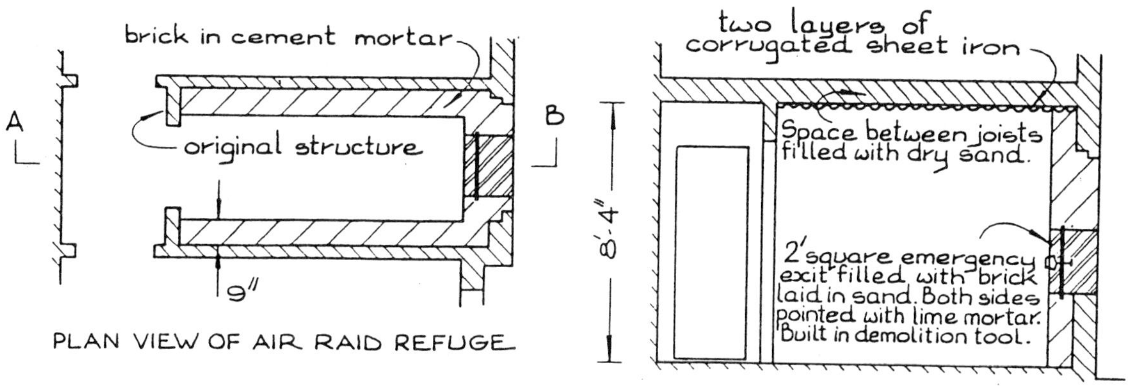

AIR RAID REFUGE CONSTRUCTED AT MESSRS BOOTS PURE DRUG CO. LTD., No. 54 HIGH STREET, STEVENAGE.

DECEMBER, 1939

Several residents living in the London Road near the Six Hills, failed to hear the air raid warning siren during a practice on the 10th, and arrangements have therefore been made for a local resident to raise the alarm using a whistle.

Many evacuees have returned home, but for those that stayed the town organised a Christmas party. The London County Council gave a grant of £10 towards the cost.

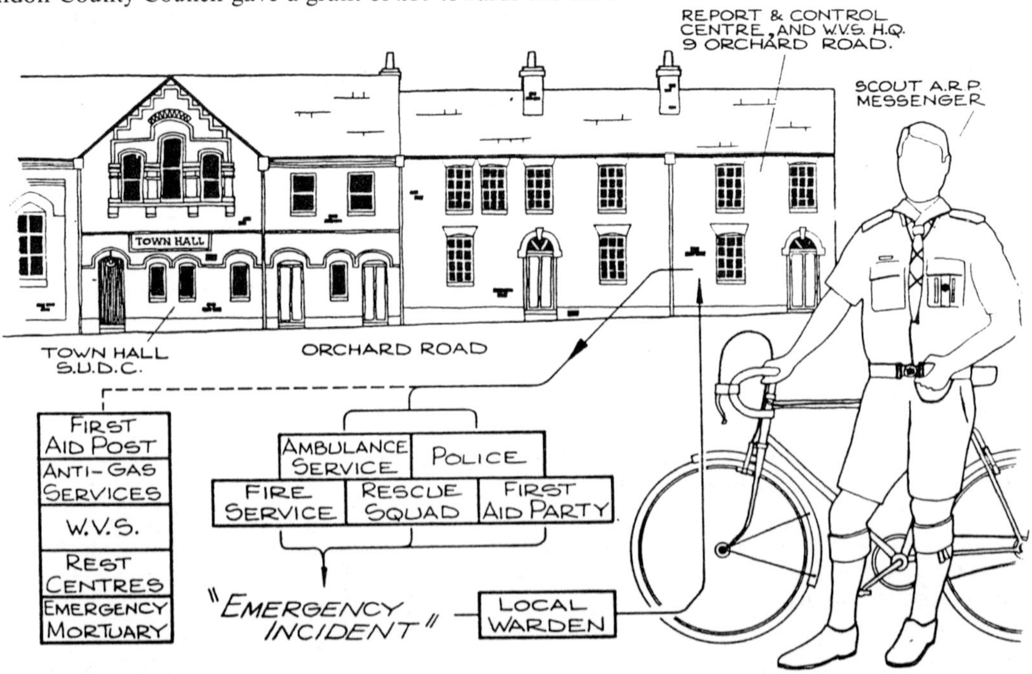

CIVIL DEFENCE EMERGENCY RESPONSE PLAN

JANUARY, 1940

Sch. Log, Jan. 8th, "School opened after the Xmas holiday. All unofficial evacuees previously attached to CHURCH STREET, STOKE NEWINGTON, attend here from today. Prior to the holiday, there was no room in this school."

Food rationing was introduced on the 8th January. Many essential commodities have become increasingly difficult to obtain. Some very welcome gifts are being received from friends overseas, as indicated by the following letter of thanks sent by the local W.V.S:-

9 Orchard Road,
Stevenage,
Herts.
ENGLAND
26th January, 1940

To the Women Golfers of Victoria Australia

Dear Ladies,

I am directed by my committee to write on behalf of the Stevenage branch of the Women's Voluntary Services for Civil Defence, to thank you most sincerely for your very thoughtful gift of cheeses.

These have been distributed to very necessitous cases in Stevenage, and the recipients wish me to pass on their very grateful thanks.

The gift is enhanced by the fact that it has travelled so many miles, bringing the thoughts of our friends so far away.

Yours sincerely,
Hon. Secretary

The two public air raid shelters, one at the north end of the High Street and one at the south end of Church Lane, are now complete. Work has begun on converting part of the cottage in the Church Lane Council premises, into a Gas Cleansing Station. The purpose of this facility is the prompt first aid treatment of blister gas casualties. It will probably consist of six sections through which the casualty will pass. First, an outside bunker into which contaminated outer clothing will be discarded; then through an air lock into an undressing room; then through a wash room with showers, baths, eye douches, etc. then through a first aid room, and finally into a dressing room. Casualties will then be taken to a local hospital for further treatment.

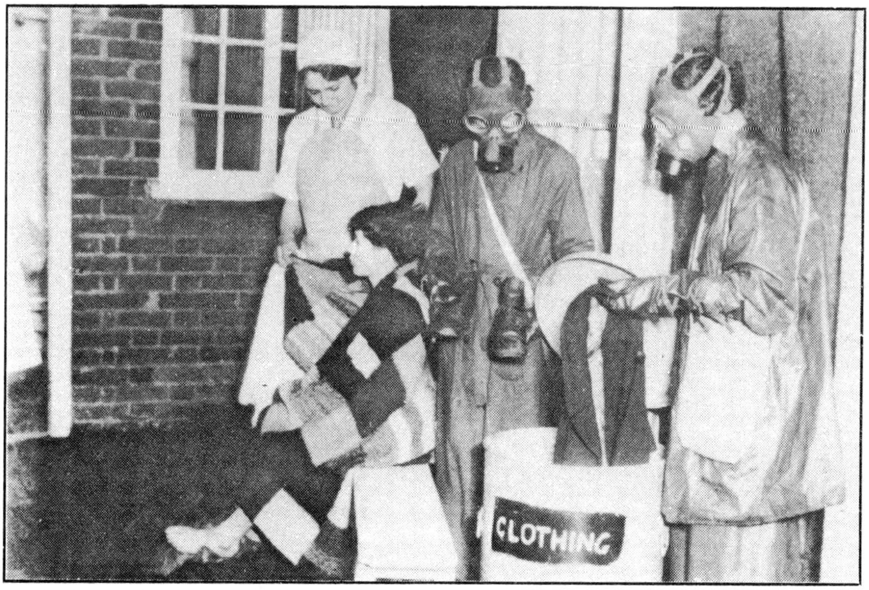

In the event of a gas attack, civilian casualties were to be given initial treatment at the First Aid Post. The casualties would have removed their clothing before entering the post for treatment, and the clothing decontaminated at a local laundry before being returned. This photograph was taken outside the post during the A.R.P. exercise held in February, 1940.
(The Pictorial)

FEBRUARY, 1940

'Black-Out' times were roughly 5.30 p.m. to 7 a.m., at the beginning of February.

The E.S.A. Sports Club presented a show by the Jabberwocks Concert Party of Bedford, in aid of their comforts fund for members serving with the forces. During the winter months, the various W.V.S. working parties produced 562 garments, which are also destined as comforts for the forces.

To relieve 'black-out boredom', members of the local Tottenham & District Gas Co.'s G.A.S. Club, have organised a series of indoor games tournaments.

The town A.R.P. Ambulance Service now have three ambulances. One is garaged at No.4 High Street, the second at No.8 and the third at Springfield House.

An additional task undertaken by the local W.V.S., is the provision of staff for the Rest Centres to be established in several halls in the town. Whilst the Rest Centres will be prepared and equipped to take in refugees at any time, the volunteers will only be called to attend in the event of an emergency. The following item was entered into the minutes of the W.V.S. meeting held on the 19th February:-

"... He (Mr. Lloyd) stated that in the event of air raids on Stevenage, it was the duty of the County Council to care for any persons rendered homeless, and to provide them with food and bedding etc.

In order to do this, the County Council had the power to requisition any hall in Stevenage; the next important item being helpers. He therefore appealed to all members of the W.V.S. to volunteer for this work of caring for the homeless, and stated in reply to a question, that help would probably only be needed for a day or two until fresh homes were found ...."

The Council estimate A.R.P. expenditure for the 1940-41 financial year to be as follows:-

A.R.P. OFFICERS SALARY	250
STATIONERY	5
RENT OF AMBULANCE SERVICE DEPOT	52
HEATING AND LIGHTING FOR ABOVE	15
RENT OF FIRST AID POST	-
HEATING AND LIGHTING FOR ABOVE	20
RENT OF REPORT AND CONTROL CENTRE	52
HEATING AND LIGHTING FOR ABOVE	30
RENT OF NO.8 HIGH STREET	26
HEATING AND LIGHTING FOR ABOVE	10
PROVISION OF GAS CLEANSING STATION	300
RENT OF GAS CLEANSING STATION	8
HEATING AND LIGHTING FOR ABOVE	7
RENT OF LAND FOR CHURCH LANE SHELTER	5
HEATING, LIGHTING AND CLEANING OF SHELTER	5
TOTAL	£785
LESS GOVERNMENT GRANT	£560
BALANCE	£225

NOTE: The salaries of full-time civil defence workers are paid by the Government.

MAY, 1940

On the 10th May, the long expected onslaught began. Enemy troops have invaded Denmark, Norway, Belgium, Luxembourg and Holland. With terrifying speed, the enemy is forcing the British and French armies to retreat towards the sea.

Also on May 10th, Neville Chamberlain resigned as Prime Minister and was succeeded by Mr. Winston Churchill. In a speech made three days later, the new Prime Minister said, "I have nothing to offer but blood, tears and sweat". There is no doubt of the danger facing Britain, and with the fall of France an invasion by enemy forces is expected at any time.

On May 14th, an appeal was made for volunteers to join an armed home defence force to be known as Local Defence Volunteers (L.D.V). Within three days, 6000 Hertfordshire men had enlisted.

Members of Stevenage Local Defence Volunteers in their denim battledress uniforms. The title was later changed to Home Guard. c1940

Stevenage A.R.P. Wardens delivering sand to householders in Fairview Road, for use in fire buckets. The W.V.S. lady accompanying the group is collecting for the Red Cross. August, 1940. (The Pictorial)

The Stevenage Local Defence Volunteers are incorporated into the 6th Company of the Hertfordshire Battalion L.D.V., which is administered by Herts. Territorial Army Association from their H.Q. in Hertford. Major General Tindall-Lucas is appointed Battalion Commander. Many of the volunteers were soldiers in the First World War and are therefore trained and experienced in much of the type of fighting thought likely to occur.

Until the L.D.V. are fully armed they can do little more than observe and report. (It has been suggested that the L.D.V. initials stand for 'look, duck and vanish'). Some of the town volunteers are being armed with timber batons cut from gymnasium wall bars made at the E.S.A. In spite of a lack of equipment the volunteers have begun serious training, and are using part of the cottage in the Church Lane Council premises as their H.Q.

The Council has provided all-weather protection for the fire appliances stationed in Whitesmead Road, Fairview Road, and Letchmore Road. Householders are to be supplied with sand for fire buckets, and also given the opportunity to buy their own stirrup pumps for £1 each.

In addition to preparations for air raids, the population is now preparing for the possibility of invasion. Many wireless broadcasts and newspaper articles are giving the general public advice on what to do. The Herts and Beds. Express dated 25th May, gave the following advice to its readers:-

> "So far as the general public is concerned, the advice given is simple but important. Anyone seeing a parachutist should report the fact at once to the nearest Police Station or L.D.V. observation post. If it is possible to keep the parachutist under observation, so much the better, but no attempt must be made to fight him or to approach enemy aircraft which have landed. In the event of air raids or parachute attacks, it is most important that all means of communication such as roads, telephones, etc. should be left clear for the defenders of the country, and civilians will help most by keeping out of the way as much as possible."

JUNE, 1940

From May 29th to June 3rd, approximately 300,000 troops, including men from Stevenage, were evacuated from the beaches of Dunkirk. France capitulated on the 17th June and now Britain stands alone. At a session of Parliament on 15th June, the Prime Minister warned that it would be folly to underrate the gravity of the impending attack. If the nation is to survive, it must win the battle for Britain likely to occur this coming summer. The phoney war seems to be over.

In order to prevent the spread of fires caused by incendiary bombs, the Council (in response to Home Office requests), are calling on residents to join street fire fighting teams. Called Supplementary Fire Parties, the teams are to be trained in elementary fire fighting using stirrup pumps. Local area wardens will prepare a census of available ladders.

The Council are also advising householders to keep buckets of water handy, and will, if requested, provide sand for fire buckets.

With the increase in military activity along the Great North Road, Stevenage has become a natural stopping place for military convoys and temporary home for a number of service personnel. A group of six new houses in Pound Avenue have been requisitioned for use as army billets, but the majority of service personnel are billeted in private accommodation. The military authorities have arranged with the Council for service personnel to use the town 'slipper baths' in Church Lane, at a cost of four pence per bath.

The Stevenage National Savings Committee oganised a savings campaign during the week 9th to 15th June, and raised £4951. A flag day was held on 15th in aid of the British Society for Sailors.

Sch. Log, June 25th, "Because of an air raid warning on the night of the 24th and the morning of the 25th, many children were absent. The warning lasted from 12.30 to 4 a.m."

JULY, 1940

The search for suitable premises to use as a forces canteen ended when Mr. and Mrs. Inns granted the W.V.S. use of the Old Castle Inn in Middle Row. Several alterations are to be made to the building (which has been empty for some time), and 35 card tables and 120 chairs are to be borrowed from the Town Hall. The canteen is to open mornings and evenings, offering simple cheap meals to visiting servicemen.

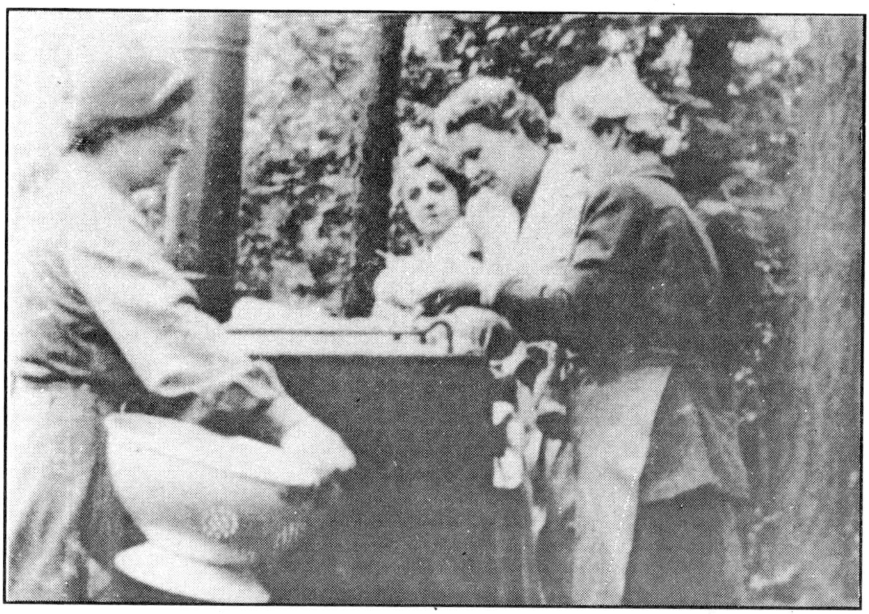

Members of the Stevenage Women's Voluntary Services training for emergency field kitchen duties. (Mrs. E. Horsfield)

The Council have supplied a trailer for use by the Rescue Party and the Decontamination Squad to transport equipment. The trailer is to be hitched to the back of a lorry provided by a local trader.

Following an appeal for aluminium by the Ministry of Aircraft Production, the Stevenage W.V.S. organised a local salvage campaign and collected just over 9 cwt of mainly household aluminium utensils. The general shortage of many raw materials has led to an almost continuous salvage campaign in which the whole community is involved. The scouts are making regular trips around the town collecting waste paper, and the Council have arranged collection points for metal, tin cans, rags and bottles, etc. A salvage bin for scrap metal has been placed in the High Street near Shelford & Crowe's Garage.

Several plots of uncultivated land in various parts of the town, are to be converted into allotments as part of the national campaign to increase the production of home grown food.

The name of the L.D.V. has changed to the Home Guard.

A private car, owned by Mr. J. Appleton, Managing Director of E.S.A., has been converted at the E.S.A. factory into an armoured vehicle by adding steel plates to the chassis. The keys of the vehicle, which is designed to carry three machine guns plus a crew of five, were presented to the Stevenage Home Guard Company Commander by Mrs. Appleton, at a parade held in the High Street on July 28th.

AUGUST, 1940

A plot of Council land in Sish Lane has been ploughed ready for use as allotments by local residents. In order to deal with the increasing problem of rats, the Hertfordshire War Agriculture Committee are offering one penny per tail for all rats destroyed. Locally, the tally of rats tails is to be verified by the Council Surveyor.

The increasing threat of air raids, has prompted several residents of Ellis Avenue to express concern for the safety of the large number of evacuee children in their area. They have asked the Council to consider providing additional shelters and to camouflage their houses.

The long expected battle for Britain began on 8th August when the enemy air force launched a series of attacks seemingly aimed at destroying the R.A.F.

The Mayor of Bexhill has written to the people of Stevenage expressing his thanks for their acceptance of evacuee children from his area.

In support of the growing national campaign to buy more Spitfires, a Stevenage Spitfire Fund has been launched with a contribution of £100 from Mr. Henderson, a local trader, and £20 from Stevenage Nurseries Ltd. As a fund raising activity, the garage proprietors, Shelford & Crowe, have organised a 'ten-a-penny' club. Club members pay one penny for every ten enemy aircraft shot down, and by 22nd August had collected £10. The daily score, which is taken from the 8 a.m. news, is chalked on the board by Mr. Furr, the High Street Fishmonger, and placed outside his shop. Within five days of being launched, the fund collected just over £454.

The first recorded enemy action near Stevenage occurred on the 30th August when a bomb was dropped in the road between Shephall and Broadwater. The explosion left a crater 20ft diameter by 4ft deep, but fortunately only a water main was damaged. Reports of incidents such as this, are recorded at the Stevenage Report and Control Centre. The entry in the records for this incident is as follows:-

"Incident Message received at Stevenage Control (abbreviated to 'Incident Message' in subsequent entries): Road between Shephall and Broadwater approx. 25 yds S. Shephall Green. H.E. Bomb. Water Main Damaged. Road still available for traffic. Size of Crater 20′ × 4′." From: HATFIELD H.C.C.

SEPTEMBER, 1940

Sch. Log, Sept. 3rd, "the air raid siren sounded at 10 a.m. The boys remained in the shelters until the all clear sounded at 11.20."

Incident Message 3/9/40 01.45, "2 Craters found at rear of Broomin Green Farm (in Orchard). Plane travelling N.W. to S.E. dropped 5 H.E. Bombs in rapid succession. The remaining 3 fell in adjacent fields. Cattle in Orchard were injured. Houses minor damaged." From: WRITTEN REPORT A.4. SECTOR.

Enemy aircraft began bombing London on 7th September.

Sch. Log, Sept. 15th, "All took to the trenches twice during the afternoon: once for 30 minutes and the other for 15 minutes."

Incident Message 15/9/40 13.28, "The German Plane which passed over Stevenage, was camouflaged as a British Wellington Bomber." From: POLICE.

Incident Message 19/9/40 02.20, "U.X.B. Pin Green 3 dropped but only one located, probably Mill Field or Keysells Field adjoining." From: B.4. SECTOR.

Incident Message 19/9/40 02.21, "Found to be H.E.'s at Sewer Farm." From: A.4. SECTOR.

Incident Message 19/9/40 03.04, "H.E. at Pin Green. Exploded. Sishes Farm 1 U.X.B. and 7 exploded." From: B.4. SECTOR.

Incident Message 19/9/40 07.50, "H.E. on bank opposite Langley Siding Signal Box." From: L.N.E.R. STEVENAGE.

Incident Message 19/9/40 09.26, "H.E. Exploded Sewage Farm direction." From: A.4. SECTOR.

Sch. Log, Sept. 19th, "Heavy bombing in the locality – many more than usual absent in the 8.55 parade. 9.30 a.m. a time bomb exploded somewhere in the vicinity: classroom doors shook. School took to the shelters from 3.40-4.10."

Incident Message 27/9/40 05.25, "Stick of Bombs dropped between Benington and Stevenage." From: WALKERN A.R.P.

Incident Message 27/9/40 07.00, "H.E. Bomb Box Wood, Walkern Road, fissures in road." From: WALKERN A.R.P.

Stevenage A.F.S. were directed to London to assist in fighting the dockland fires.

Members of the Stevenage First Aid Party loading a 'casualty' into an ambulance during the A.R.P. exercise held in February, 1940. Note that the First Aid Party includes members of the St. John Ambulance Brigade. This photograph was taken in Basil's Road, alongside the First Aid Post, and looking towards Church Lane. (The Pictorial)

OCTOBER, 1940

Incident Message 1/10/40 00.02,"2 Parachute Mines vicinity Oakfield Cottages, minor damage to Cottages. Broken shop windows Stevenage." From: A.4. SECTOR.

Incident Message 1/10/40 07.12,"2 Parachute Mines (1) 800 yds N.W. Philpots House Broomin Green Farm. (2) Due South Gates Farm East side of Road." From: STEVENAGE POLICE.

Incident Message 1/10/40 12.55, "It is known that 4 oil bombs exploded in last nights raid ¾ mile away due west." From: STEVENAGE POLICE.

The Anti-Aircraft Brigade mobile concert party, presented a show called "Go To It" at the Town Hall in aid of the Troop Welfare Fund. The show included the all girl sextet "The Six Spitfires." On Sunday the 6th, the Stevenage and District Spitfire Fund Committee present an "All Star Concert" at the Astonia Cinema featuring several local performers.

Incident Message 7/10/40 20.30,"Stick of H.E.'s at Fairlands Farm. U.X.B's suspected." From: FAIRLANDS FARM.

Incident Message 7/10/40 20.55, "1 H.E. situated N. end of field No. 25. Ord: 1 H.E. North end field 8 Ord: 1 Flame Oil Bomb N. end fields 22 × 23 Ord." From: SHEPHALL A.R.P.

Sch. Log Oct. 3rd, "The school took to the trenches at 9.30 and came out at 10.53, cold and wet. Took shelter again at 11.10. All clear at 11.50. Siren at 1.35 p.m. All clear at 5.00 p.m. No registration in the afternoon as most boys remained at home."

Sch. Log Oct. 4th, "Siren sounded at 1.30 and so many not present by 1.40 the time for assembly. Shelter taken from 3.00 until 3.12."

Sch. Log Oct. 14th, "Time of the assembly ...... deranged by reason of the siren sounding at 1.15. School dismissed at 12.30 p.m."

Incident Message 15/10/40 01.15, "H.E's in direction of Shephall." From: KNEBWORTH A.R.P.

Incident Message 16/10/40 22.30,"A delayed action bomb believed to be near refuse dump, Fishers Green." From: A.2. POST.

Incident Message 17/10/40 00.50, "Unconfirmed report of U.X.B. at Todds Green." From: HITCHIN A.R.P.

Incident Message 20/10/40 23.50, "Stick of H.E.'s dropped in direction of Shephall. 1 U.X.B." From: A.5. SECTOR.

Incident Message 20/10/40 23.55, "22 U.X.B's near Sewer Farm 23.50. Explosions heard toward Shephall previous." From: A.4. SECTOR.

Incident Message 20/10/40, "Confirmed. 4 H.E.'s Loves Wood (1 U.X.B)." From: SHEPHALL A.R.P.

Sch. Log Oct. 31st, "The siren went at 12.55 and the all clear at 3.10 p.m. It rained .... all the 'dinner' period and throughout all the afternoon. Attendance very poor. Number of pupils present on Thursday p.m. 85 Herts. boys and 2 unofficial evacuees."

NOVEMBER, 1940

The Council bought 6 mattresses, 6 single blankets, 18 coloured blankets, 12 pillows, 18 pillowslips, and 6 waterproof sheets for use at the Fire Station. The location of the three A.F.S. trailer pumps has been changed again. One pump is to be stationed at 8 High Street (a premises being used as an A.R.P. equipment store),

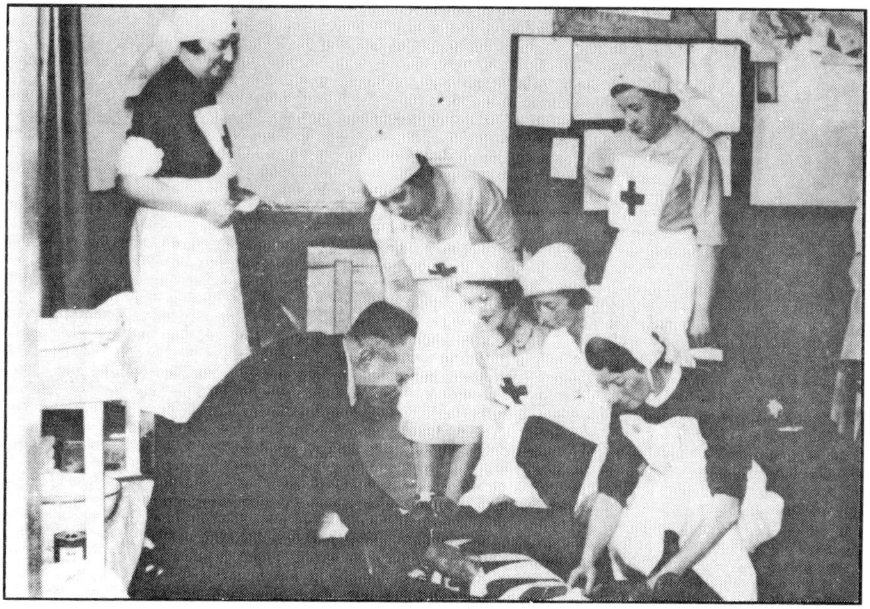

Stevenage Red Cross nurses on duty at the town First Aid Post during the A.R.P. exercise held on the 24th February, 1940. Also seen in the photograph is Dr. Skeggs the post Medical Officer.
(The Pictorial)

one at the Stevenage Motor Co., and the third at the Fire Station in Basil's Road. Garaging for the three A.R.P. ambulances has been moved from 48A High Street (the shop is about to be let), to 52A High Street. The sandbag walls protecting the First Aid Post, the Fire Station, and the Ambulance Depot, are all in a poor state of repair and the Council have decided to replace them with brick protection screens. Additional protection has been provided for those houses being used as A.R.P. Wardens Posts (eg. 14 Southsea Road). The disused gas holder at the Sish Lane Gas Works, is to be filled with water as a reserve supply for fire fighting.

Sch. Log Nov. 5th, "Trenches leaked very badly but the rainfall during the weekend was torrential."

Sch. Log Nov. 20th, "School given a half holiday to enable the senior boys to see a football match in Stevenage in aid of the Spitfire Fund."

JANUARY, 1941

The Stevenage National Savings Committee report that the town collected £126,190 during 1940.

Incident Message 20/1/41 16.20, "Single Enemy Aircraft Dornier 215 came from direction of Hitchin and circled westward of Kings factory crossing the railway, circled back again and made off up the line to Hitchin. When passing Fishers Green Bridge going N. it made a shallow dive, and something appeared to drop out." From: E.S.A. SPOTTER.

Four local people appeared at Stevenage Police Court on Thursday 23rd and were fined for contravention of the black-out regulations. Mrs. A of London Road was fined 30s. The reporting constable stated that the black-out material used did not quite cover the windows. Mrs. B of Benington was fined 15s with 6s costs for allowing an unscreened window. This was reported by a member of the Home Guard. Mr. C. of Stevenage High Street was fined 10s for poor screening of his shop window. This was reported by a member of the Police War Reserve. Mrs. D of Stevenage High Street was fined 10s with 11s 6d cost for allowing a light to show in her house.

Sch. Log Jan. 31st, "The siren went at 1.10 p.m. Registers kept open until 2.15. The senior boys generally attended. Many junior boys absent. Those attendances included in the weekly percentages return. All clear sounded at 3.30. 156 boys present out of 251.

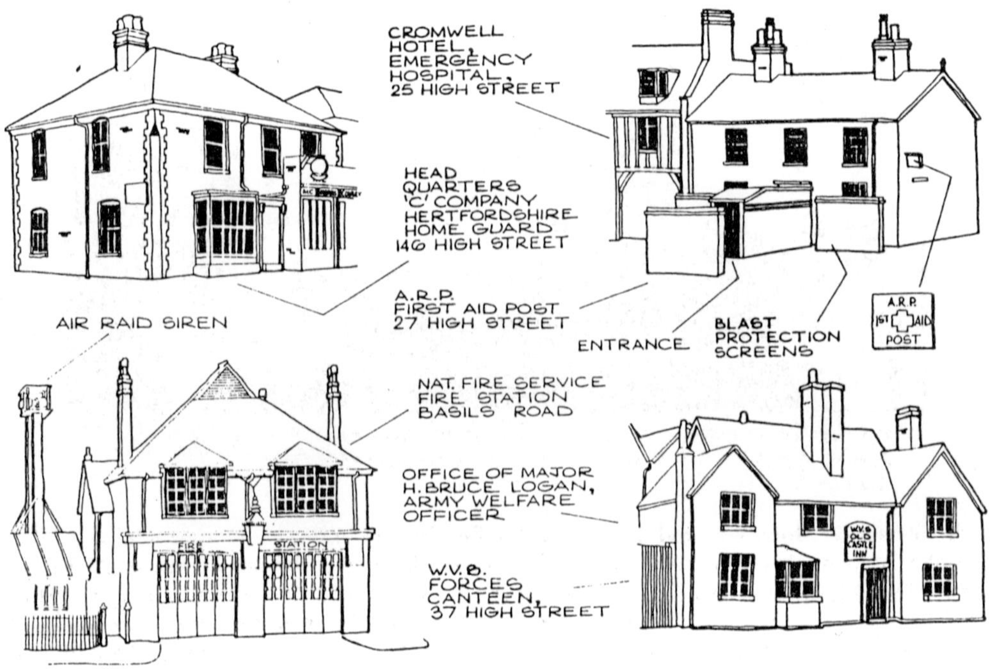

FEBRUARY, 1941

Incident Message 14/2/41 21.15, "Canister of I.B's between 'Cherry Tree' and Oakley Farm including Mobbs Bury, no damage." From: DR. DORY, MOBBS BURY.

MARCH, 1941

A coal ration of 1 cwt per week, is to be allowed for use at the Wardens Post at 87 Haycroft Road.

The following advertisement appeared in The Pictorial dated March 11th:-

"HERTS WAR AGRICULTURAL EXECUTIVE COMMITTEE"
County Hall Hertford
WOMEN'S EMERGENCY LAND CORPS
A call to women to help their country.
URGENTLY WANTED

Volunteers to enrol and work in this locality when needed, whole days and half days, or evenings, for weeding, hoeing, singling, pea picking, haymaking, harvesting, potato and root lifting, fruit picking etc. Payment at current wage rates per hour or piecework. For further information apply Mrs. Gray, Organiser, Women's Emergency Land Corps, County Hall, Hertford."

Sch. Log Mar. 12th, "Firewatching began here. Details of the scheme were forwarded to the County Council and approved."

NOTE: The Fire Watchers Order, introduced last September, requires a patrol system to be operated in prescribed areas and premises, particularly at night, in order to detect fire and raise the alarm.

Sch. Log Mar. 31st, "Equipment intended for use at the Technical Instruction Centre in time of emergency communual feeding, arrived. This equipment is stored in the school stock room and consists of:-

100 meal plates	100 soup spoons	100 beakers
100 dessert knives	100 dessert forks	100 teaspoons
100 dessert spoons		

Stevenage War Weapons Week began with a parade on Saturday 22nd, which included contingents of the local Civil Defence units, the Home Guard, the Army, and the R.A.F. The salute was taken by Lord Hampden (Lord Lieutenant of the County) from a platform erected outside the Stevenage Club and Insitute. Also on the platform were: Mr. Marsden Popple (Chief Warden), Major G. Sherriff, Lady Hampden and Maj-Gen. G.E. Tindall Lucas C.B. The target set by the organising committee is £30,000, the cost of two medium tanks.

A man living at Fishers Green was acquitted at Stevenage Police Court following a charge of failing to immobilize his unattended car. He stated that he was only 25 yds away and had the car in view all the time. (The Motor Vehicles Control Order 1940, requires mechanically propelled vehicles to be immobilized if left unattended).

APRIL, 1941

The Council are to place salvage bins in each street, to collect scraps of food for feeding pigs.

The Stevenage A.F.S. bought a motor cycle for £12 to aid communication, and the Rescue Party bought a lorry for £85.

Mr. Greenwood, the local St. John Ambulance Brigade Officer, is to attend an Air Raid Incident Officers course.

MAY, 1941

The Council advised householders that they can be given help in the strengthening of their 'refuge room'.

Note: Householders are advised to choose and prepare one room in which they can take cover during an air raid. The room should be strengthened and sealed against gas, and contain a supply of essential stores. An emergency supply of food, extra clothing, a First Aid kit, and a comprehensive selection of household items including a tin-opener and chamber-pot are recommended.

Incident Message 24/5/41 03.39, "Flare 30deg: N. 5-7 miles away." From: E.S.A. SPOTTER.

JUNE, 1941

The Council received numerous complaints about the damage caused by dogs roaming the town allotments, and are to erect notices stating that the owners of the dogs causing the nuisance could be fined £5 under Section 62AA of the Defence General Regulations. The Council erected the following notice as a warning to trespassers:-

URBAN DISTRICT COUNCIL
NOTICE
DEFENCE REGULATIONS
THIS LAND IS CULTIVATED AS ALLOTMENT GARDENS. NOTICE IS HEREBY GIVEN THAT IF ANY PERSON TRESPASSES ON THIS LAND HE SHALL, UNDER REGULATION 61(2) OF THE DEFENCE REGULATIONS, BE GUILTY OF AN OFFENCE AGAINST THIS REGULATION AND LIABLE, ON SUMMARY CONVICTION, TO A FINE NOT EXCEEDING £50

Mr. Mott has resigned as Senior Warden of Sector A4.

The Council accepted an estimate of £188 to erect two A.R.P. Wardens Posts.

The parish of Ardeley has been transferred from Stevenage to the Buntingford A.R.P. administration area.

Sch. Log. June 20th, "The school canteen is now definitely overcrowded: over 150 attend each day."

Arrangements have been made for Fire Watchers to use the St. John Ambulance brigade hut at Six Hills.

The Council accepted an estimate of £11-16-3, to provide additional protection for the A.R.P. Wardens Post at 87 Haycroft Road.

JULY, 1941

An additional air raid shelter is to be provided for the residents of Primrose Hill Road and Ditchmore Common.

Four mattresses costing £9 and four chairs costing £4, have been bought by the Council for use at the Wardens Posts being erected at Fairview Road and Whitesmead Road.

Incident Message 14/7/41 02.25, "Knebworth Machine Gunned by Enemy Plane, 4 casualties. Also Red Cross Train machine gunned at Langley Siding, small damage to train." From: KNEBWORTH CONTROL.

NOTE: To facilitate evacuation of patients from hospitals in cities which are liable to receive heavy raids, a number of specially adapted trains have been berthed at strategic locations about the country. The trains, known as Casualty Evacuation Trains, consist of 12 coaches comprising 2 brake vans, 9 stretcher vans, and a staff and kitchen car. They can accommodate approximately 300 stretcher cases and carry fire fighting equipment as well as food and medical supplies. The permanent crew attached to each train (generally billeted in local accommodation), comprise a medical officer in charge, 3 trained nurses, 10 auxiliary nurses, and 8 orderlies. The trains were initially used during the first few days of the war, and then after almost a year of inactivity were again used during the

Members of the Stevenage National Fire Service with their fire engine (an Austin Towing Vehicle) and trailer pump. The National Fire Service was formed in August 1941, and superseded the earlier Auxiliary Fire Service. c1943. (P. Howard)

Battle of Britain and the Blitz. One of the dozen or so trains serving the London area, is berthed at Langley Siding. A few of the crew members working on this train are registered as Conscientious Objectors.

AUGUST, 1941

Following the considerable difficulties experienced during the Blitz of co-ordinating the activities of a multitude of different fire fighting authorities, all using different equipment, the Government decided to nationalize the fire services. On August 18th, all existing fire authorities, including the Stevenage A.F.S. and town volunteer fire brigade, were amalgamated into a National Fire Service.

SEPTEMBER, 1941

The Home Office notified all local government authorities (Home Office Circular 174.1941) that a fire prevention organisation to be known as the Fire Guard, is to be established as part of the A.R.P. services. Experience during the Blitz has shown that a small number of enemy aircraft can, in just a few minutes, shower a town with thousands of incendiary bombs. If not tackled promptly, the number of large fires likely to result would almost certainly be beyond the control of the available fire fighting services. The purpose of the Fire Guard is to deal promptly with incendiary bombs wherever they fall. Since the two services are to work in close co-operation, the Fire Guard organisation has been constituted as part of the A.R.P. Warden Service and their operational boundaries will generally coincide. The Fire Guards, who will be mainly volunteers, are to be grouped into Stirrup Pump Teams consisting of three persons. In built-up areas there will be at least one 'watching team' on duty (particularly at night) for every 150 yds. of street, or for every 30 houses if there are more than 30 houses in the 150 yds. Team rotas are to be arranged to spread the watching duties over as many members as possible. A whistle is to be used by the duty team to alert off duty members and the general public of a fall of bombs. Where necessary the Fire Guard are enpowered to enter buildings for the purpose of extinguishing fire, protecting property, or rescuing persons. They will be trained in general A.R.P. work and elementary first aid, as well as fire fighting techniques.

The Home Office notified all local government authorities, that the name A.R.P. Services has been officially changed to the Civil Defence Services. The name of the Stevenage A.R.P. Committee has therefore changed to the Stevenage Civil Defence Committee.

OCTOBER, 1941

The Council are to conduct a survey of the town to find iron railings etc. which could be removed for salvage. It is not proposed to remove structures such as gates etc., where it would be necessary to replace them with some other material.

The Clearance of Lofts Act 1940, directs local authorities to inspect all lofts in their district, to ensure that they are cleared of articles not affixed to the premises. (Excluding lofts used for human habitation). The Council have requested the local N.F.S. to exercise this duty. This requirement resulted from experience during the Blitz, when many buildings were destroyed by incendiary bombs that had fallen into lofts packed with jumble etc. (The order to enter and inspect private premises is obviously very unpopular, and the Council are experiencing considerable difficulty in persuading anyone to undertake this task).

The Herts. County Council agreed that ambulances may be used for duties other than A.R.P. tasks resulting from enemy action, provided they are kept in good working order.

The staff of the Orchard Restaurant, which opened in the Town Hall on Wednesday the 22nd, served their first meal to approximately 50 children. The menu comprised stewed steak, carrots and potatoes, with jam tart and custard to follow. The restaurant, which is staffed by volunteers and managed by Captain A.J. Templeton, has been organised by the Welfare Committee as part of the British Restaurant scheme. The restaurant will be open six days per week and meals will cost 4d for children and 8d for adults. The volunteer helpers are Miss Bennett, Miss Banks, Mrs. Clarke, Miss Fell, Mrs. Cantor and Mrs. Pollock. The British Restaurants have been developed from the Government plans to feed the civil population during any emergency which disrupts normal facilities. Home cooking has become increasingly more difficult as more and more women are recruited into the factories, etc. The British restaurants together with the growing number of school and factory canteens, are providing people with at least one hot meal per day. The meals are simple, nutritious and cheap, and are in addition to the authorised food ration.

Sch. Log October, "Many boys absent in the potato fields. A great shortage of labour – women usually employed are now in factories. Prior to this harvest, the number of attendances was over 92. The average for October is just over 80."

NOVEMBER, 1941

The Council have requested the military authorities to pay for the damage caused to The Avenue by military vehicles.

Re. the Clearance of Lofts Act 1940, the Council requested the town Sanitary Inspector to exercise this duty.

A sub-committee of the Council Civil Defence Committee, formed to establish the town Fire Guard Service, resolved that the structure of the service shall be as follows: a Fire Guard Staff Officer, a Head Fire Guard, and 10 Senior Fire Guards to correspond to the 10 Senior A.R.P. Wardens. The Fire Guards are to operate the same town sector divisions as the Wardens.

The Stevenage, Knebworth and District Warship Week, is to be launched by a parade in the High Street and a concert at the Astonia on Sunday the 30th. The target of £62,000 set by the Committee, is for a Trawler-Minesweeper.

DECEMBER, 1941

The Council Highways and Lighting Committee received a complaint from a resident who fell over some kerbstones at the junction of London Road and Trinity Road. The Committee are to pass the complaint to the Home Guard who own the kerbstones.

The Stevenage Welfare Committee are to arrange a Christmas Party for evacuee children billeted in the town. The party is to be held at the Town Hall.

Sch. Log Dec. 19th, "School closed for Xmas Holidays. Total war savings for the term £355.15.0. Total during Navy Week £160."

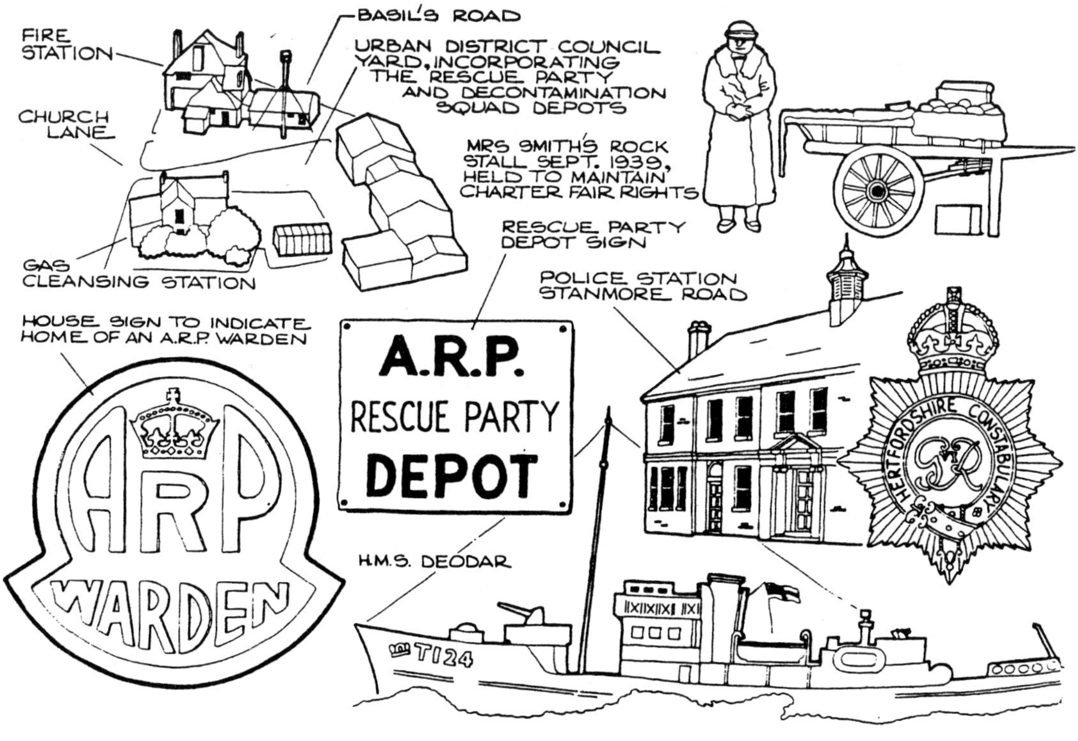

JANUARY, 1942

The Council report that the number of evacuees billeted in the town is now 535. During December last, 36 evacuees left the town and 5 arrived. It was also reported that number 63 Letchmore Road had been requisitioned for evacuees.

The Stevenage National Savings Committee report that the town raised £181,367 during 1941.

The following advertisement appeared in the Hertfordshire Pictorial dated January 27th:

> "HOMEWORK. Will ladies in the Stevenage district who are unable to work in factories, and who are willing to take on work in their own homes, please communicate with: MISS D. GROSVENOR, HIGH STREET, STEVENAGE.

The Council announced the following appointments in the new Fire Guard service:

Fire Guard Staff Officer, Mr. A.E. Gray
Head Fire Guard, Mr. H. King, 1 Nottingham Road
Senior Fire Guard, Sector A2, Mr. H. Warren, 18 Essex Road
A3, Mr. H. Oxley, 14 Julians Road
A4, Mr. W. Burgess, 115 Fairview Road
A5, Mr. W.A. Walker, Cherry Wood, Bedwell Lane
B2, Mr. J. Pedley, 100 Letchmore Road
B3, Mr. T. Kane, 80 Haycroft Road
B4, Mr. F. Ashworth, 30 Lawrence Avenue
B5, Mr. L.G. Wiggins, 129 Walkern Road

Recommendations were not made at this time for Sectors A1 and B1. 525 Fire Guards have enrolled to man the sectors.

It has been reported that the Wardens Post in Fairview Road is suffering from condensation.

FEBRUARY, 1942

The Home Guard have been granted permission to use the temporary mortuary at the Sish Lane Gas Works as a miniature rifle range.

The Fire Guard Service obtained additional helmets, armlets and whistles, to bring the total number of each to 650. They have also added 25 stirrup pumps to their collection of equipment.

A Stevenage Fire Guard team in action during the invasion exercise held in 1942. The signs on the front and side of the A.R.P. ambulance, contain the intials "ARP", a red cross, and the legend "1st. Aid Party". (The Pictorial)

A recent dance held at the Town Hall was organised by No.7 Platoon Home Guard in aid of the Prisoners of War Fund, and Hitchin Hospital are to benefit from a dance arranged by the Stevenage Fire Service Social Club. A collection made at the Stevenage churches raised £16 in aid of the Red Cross.

To economise on the use of fuel, tyres, manpower, etc, the Government are asking retail traders to pool their transport services for the collection and delivery of goods. A local organising committee is to be formed comprising: Messrs. C.C. Grimshaw, S. Jones, C.H. Mott, H. O'Clee, W.G. Nichols, E. Henderson and H.J. Hutchinson, with C.A. Day as Chairman.

MARCH, 1942

The Tottenham & District Gas Co. granted the Fire Guard Service permission to use a garage on their premises at 70 High Street as an equipment store.

Many townsfolk are contributing to the R.A.F. Benevolent Fund via a home collection scheme known as "Raiders Passed."

Sch. Log, March 25th, "Mr. Slow superintended the testing of all gas masks in the Gas Chamber on Bury Mead (2-3.30)"

A group of local Tottenham and District Gas Company employees, who were also members of the Home Guard or the Rescue Party/Gas (RP/G). In the event of an air raid, the RP/G workers were responsible for making safe damaged gas installations. This was one of the most dangerous civil defence duties. c1942.

Over £105 was raised for Mrs. Churchill's Aid to Russia Fund via a dance held at the E.S.A. Pavilion on Saturday 14th.

The Regional Commissioner has requested local government authorities together with the military, police, fire and food authorities, to prepare for the eventuality of an invasion. The Council Emergency Committee submitted the following plan to the Hertfordshire County A.R.P. Headquarters:-

STEVENAGE URBAN DISTRICT COUNCIL
CIVIL INVASION PLAN

1. The addresses and telephone numbers of Chairman and members of the Emergency Committee, together with co-opted members, and officials charged with executive duties, are shown in Appendix (A).

2. The geographical area covered by the plan is Stevenage Urban District and the approximate population is 7,000.

3. Resources of local authority, headquarters of services, with alternative accommodation, names of executive officers and their deputies, are shown in Appendix (B).

4. Alternative methods of communication, in the event of telephone services being disrupted, are shown in Appendix (C).

5. A copy of a leaflet to be issued to all householders telling them what the Committee has done, is doing, and will do, and what the public should do, is given in Appendix (D).

6. **Co-operation with Military**

On "Action Stations" the Senior Military Representative will arrange for military liaison officer Lieut. Wilson to report to Control Centre. Civil Defence Controller will arrange for a C.D. official to report to Military Headquarters. Plan when completed should be signed by the Chairman of Emergency Committee and Senior Military representative.

7. **Homeless and Refugees**

Some refugees are bound to drift into district. Arrangements for their accommodation and for accommodating people rendered homeless by enemy action or by orders of Police or Military Authorities must be made.

A list of Rest Centres, together with names of officers-in-charge, is shown in Appendix (E).

Notice boards indicating location of Rest Centres will be erected and sited with a view to getting people off main roads as quickly as possible.

8. **Instructions to Public**

Morale can best be maintained by manning essential services to the last and providing a job for everybody.

Panic can be prevented by similar methods and by keeping the population fully informed of the situation and measures taken to deal with it. Services should combat rumour and set an example by their bearing.

The Ministry of Information bulletin boards and official notice-boards have been erected as per Appendix (F).

This informatation will be supplemented by special broadcasts by B.B.C and official orders given through Police and Wardens Service by heads of these Services.

9. **Fire**

Fire appliances and static water are located as per Appendix (G). N.F.S. have devised a comprehensive mutual assistance scheme.

10. **Hygiene**

Water. In the event of main water supply being cut alternative arrangements for supply of water are shown in Appendix (H).

Latrines. Improved latrine arrangements should be made in accordance with Appendix (I).

Mortuary. Arrangements are shown in Appendix (J).

11. **Clearance of Debris and Road Repair**

It is essential to keep military roads open. Labour and tools must be immediately available to clear debris, fill in craters, etc. Priority of work decided by military. All able-bodied persons liable to be called on for this work. Detailed plans for organising working parties are shown in Appendix (K).

12. **Food**

All food supplies in the district will, if necessary, be requisitioned and distributed to the military and civil population under orders of the Food Executive Officer. Details of approximate quantities of food available are shown in Appendix (L).

13. **Medical Services**

Details of Medical Officers and Medical Units available in the district are shown in Appendix (M) together with lists of buildings, houses, etc. which have been earmarked for use as First Aid Posts or Points.

14. **Decontamination**

Details of cleansing Stations are given in Appendix (N).

15. **Schools**

Consideration has been given to the welfare of school children in the event of schools being closed. A small committee of headmasters and mistresses will be appointed to consider and report on this matter.

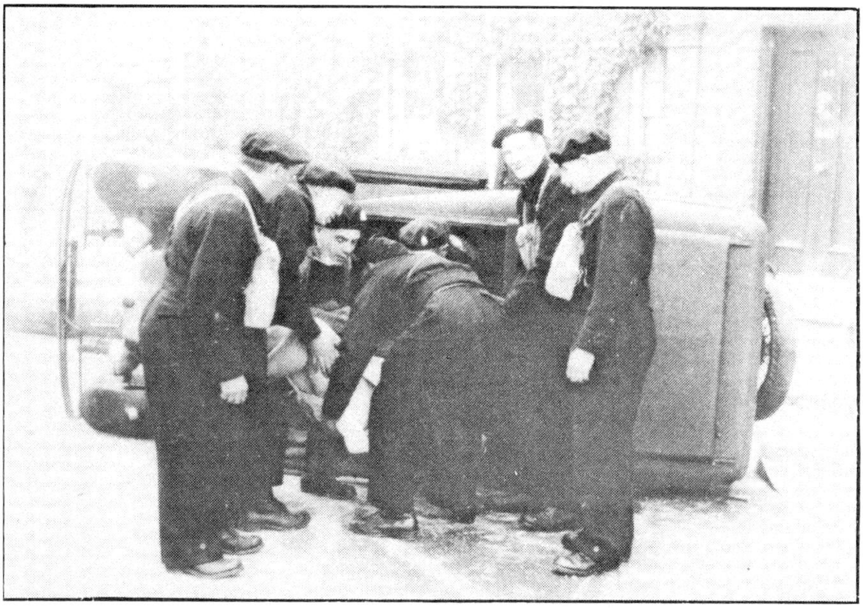

A Stevenage Rescue Squad in action during the invasion exercise held in 1942. This photograph was taken outside No. 68 High Street *(The Pictorial)*

APPENDIX TO CIVIL INVASION PLAN

(A) Members of Emergency Committee, Associated Members, Officials, etc.

Mr. J.A. Marsden Popple, (Chairman) Danes Hill. (Tel. 48)
Mr. F.J. Blow, 44 Basils Road
Mr. W.E. Conlin, 103 Walkern Road
Mr. J.H. Reeves, 'Berkeley', London Road. (Tel. 159)
Mr. W. Sherriff, 11 Essex Road. (Tel. 409)
Mr. R.H. Walker, 4 Essex Road. (Tel. 246)
Maj. Gen. C.H. Tindall Lucas, Northwood. (Tel. 126)
(Senior Military Representative)
Mr. A.G. Ridgon, 26 High Street. (Tel. 234) (M of Food Office)
(Food Executive Officer)
Inspector F. Futter, Police Station. (Tel. 58)
Mr. B.F. Rolph, Fire Station. (Tel. 192)
(Fire Service Section Leader)
Mr. A. Primett, Council Offices. (Tel. 302)
(A.R.P. Controller)

(B) Headquarters of Services, Executive Officers, etc

Report & Control Centre, Mr. P.T. Ireton, Officer in Charge (Tel 237)
First Aid Post, Dr. B.L. Skeggs, Doctor in Charge (Tel. 251)
Ambulance and First Aid Party Depot, Mr. F.L.W. Slow,
Ambulance Office Officer (Tel. 74)
Cleansing Station, Mr. Reg. A. Gandy, Surveyor (Tel. 393)
A.R.P. Officer, Mr. R.P. Flint, 7 Orchard Road (Tel. 302)
Billeting Officer, Mr. H. Smeaton, 9 Orchard Road (Tel. 302)
Rest Centres, Rev. L.F. Higgs, 69 Basils Road

(C) Alternative Methods of Communications

By messengers.

(D) Information to the Public – Copy Leaflet

PLAN

Comprehensive plans have been made by the Emergency Committee of your Council in consultation with representatives of the Military, Police, Fire, Food and Labour Services, which will be put into effect in the event of this country being invaded or an attempt at invasion being made.

BOMBING

Heavy bombing may be expected to precede attempted invasion. The Military, including the Home Guard, will, during this period, augment your regular Civil Defence Services.

PARATROOPS

Enemy paratroops may be landed as a next stage to disrupt communications and to seize aerodromes or ground suitable for landing enemy air-borne troops. These will be summarily dealt with by Military and Home Guard.

MILITARY

Home Guard and Civil Defence Services will be mustered as soon as danger threatens. Martial law comes into operation on invasion and you should fully realise that instant obedience to orders of the military and civil authorities must be unquestioning and that refusal results in severe penalties even to the extreme.

FOOD

There are adequate food supplies in the district to maintain the civil population for a considerable time. Arrangements have been made for equible distribution. Where necessary, additional communal kitchens will be opened.

WATER

If normal supply fails, there is sufficient water in the District to last for many days on a basis of one gallon per head per day. You should exercise the strictest economy of its use from the first.

LATRINE

If the water supply fails or sewers are damaged, latrines should be dug in gardens as far from houses as possible or receptacles in the house should be emptied into holes at least two feet deep in gardens. A number of latrines for general use will be provided if necessary.

REST CENTRES

Rest Centres for reception of people rendered homeless by enemy action will be opened and staffed continuously. The way to them will be signposted. Good neighbourliness will go a long way to solving the problem of the homeless.

MEDICAL

If necessary, additional First Aid Points and Emergency Hospitals will be established. They will be clearly marked with a Red Cross.

GAS

If the enemy use gas and you become contaminated, remove contaminated clothing and wash affected parts of the body. The greatest protection against gas, especially spray, is to stay indoors. Facilities for decontamination are provided at the First Aid Post, 27 High Street.

WORKING PARTIES

Much unskilled labour may be required for preparing defences, digging trenches, removing debris, repairing roads, etc. Every able-bodied person is bound by law to assist. Don't wait to be pressed. Volunteer at once.

INFORMATION

News Bulletins and instructions to the public will be put up on official notice boards which are at the Town Hall, Post Offices (3), Police Station, Holy Trinity Church and Esavian Works. Study these instructions. Ignorance of orders is no excuse.

KEEP OFF MAIN ROADS so as not to hinder military traffic and operations.

DON'T PANIC - It won't do you or anyone else any good.

Keep on with your ordinary job as long as possible. When that is impossible find something to do. If you are busy doing something useful, you will not have time to worry.

(E) **Rest Centres and Officers in Charge**

Town Hall, Orchard Road - Mrs. J.A. Marsden Popple (W.V.S)
Bunyan Baptist School Room, Basils Road - Mrs. L.F. Higgs
Parish Hall, Basils Road - Rev. K.H. Hart
Alleyne's Grammer School Hall - Mr. K.P. Thorpe
Church of England School - Mrs. Carr, 10 Bridge Road
C.C. School, Letchmore Road - Mr. W.H. Roach, 37 Fishers Green Road

(F) **Official Notice Boards**

Police Station, Stanmore Road
Post Office, High Street
Town Hall, Orchard Road
Sub-Post Office, Whitesmead Road
Holy Trinity Church, High Street
Esavian Works, Fishers Green Road

(G) **Fire Appliances and Static Water Supplies**

Fire Appliances at Fire Station, Church Lane and Garage, 8 High Street

Static Water Supplies:-

5,000 gallon steel tank, Car Park, High Street
Disused gas holder, Sish Lane
Ponds on land adjoining Fishers Green
Esavian Sports Ground, Fairview Road

(H) **Alternative Water Supplies**

A schedule of wells in the District has been prepared. Distribution would be made by means of water carts. Residents will be instructed to fill baths and all other available receptacles when invasion is imminent, and to boil all water not drawn from normal services.

(I) **Improvised Latrine Arrangements**

Residents will be requested to provide latrines on all suitable private premises and a number of latrines for general use will be provided.

(J) **Mortuary Arrangements**

An emergency mortuary has been provided and equipped at the Gas Works, Letchmore Road.

(K) **Organisation of Working Parties**

Returns obtained from employers show labour and tools to be available as follows:-

Men 129, Horses 24, Picks 92, Shovels 116, Forks 97.

(L) **Food Supplies**

Stocks Available

Adequate supplies are distributed over the country to provide food for a considerable period.

Retailers have an average of two weeks reserve.

Certain named traders are holding supplies belonging to the Ministry of Food.

There are stocks in local storage and adjacent towns.

On "Action Stations", the Food Executive Officer will furnish to the Emergency Committee, a list of the stocks which can be indented upon to replenish retailers depleted, so long as conditions allow.

On the order **"stand to"**, instructions may be issued to the public restricting purchases to one week.

On the order **"action stations"**, the Food Executive Officer will issue an order to all retailers and catering establishments to close for three hours for the purpose of making stock returns to the Food Officer.

The Food Executive Officer will summarise all stocks and determine the rations allowance to be in force per head of the registered population.

Unrationed Foods

The weekly amount which the public will be permitted to purchase, will be determined in terms of cash.

Poster notices will be displayed in all food shops accordingly and the shops and establishments instructed to re-open and carry on in the normal way.

Bread and Milk - deliveries will cease.

Distribution will be made from depots opened and situated in various localities controlled by deputies appointed by the respective Area Contact Officers of the Ministry.

Tradesmen may inform their customers in advance where they may obtain supplies. Notices will be posted in the respective areas. Householders must take their ration books and pay cash. In cases of destitute persons, bread and milk will be given on the authority of the Public Assistance Officer.

The rations and prices will be determined as circumstances demand.

Milk

The marking on page 11 of the yellow ration book will be used to enforce a milk ration under emergency.

Requisitioning of Food

On advice from the Senior Military Representative warranting such action, the Food Executive Officer will exercise the power vested in him by the Ministry of Food, to requisition and distribute to the general public, as equitably as possible, all the stocks of human foodstuffs held by the retailers.

(M) **Medical Services**

Dr. B. Suggit (Medical Officer of Health) Council Offices (Tel. 302)
Dr. D. Pike, 66 High Street (Tel. 52)
Dr. B.L. Skeggs, 9 High Street (Doctor in Charge of First Aid Post) (Tel. 27)
First Aid Post, 27 High Street (Tel. 251)
First Aid Party Depot, 31 High Street (Tel. 74)
Emergency Hospital, Cromwell Hotel

(N) **Cleansing Stations**

First Aid Post, 27 High Street (Tel. 261) for General Public.
Depot, Church Lane (Tel. 323) for Uniformed Personnel

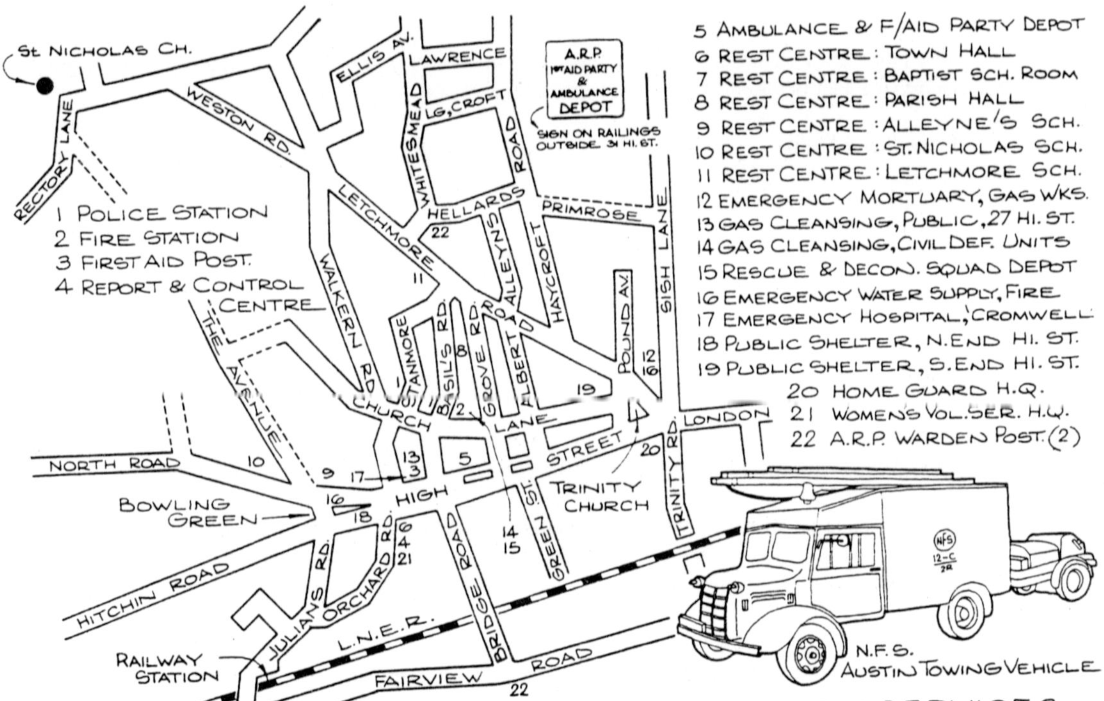

LOCATION MAP – EMERGENCY SERVICES

The following military plan was prepared by Stevenage Home Guard in response to the Regional Commissioners request:-

HOME GUARD DEFENCE SCHEME - STEVENAGE

1. INFORMATION

The town of Stevenage consists mainly of one long main street ie. Great North Road. At the northern end the road divides into two, forming a narrow fork. At the southern end there is a large 5 cross roads.

The problem of defence resolves itself into the best method of holding the main road. This can be easily achieved by siting the Keep at the 5 cross roads, which is also the site of the Home Guard Company H.Q., with a D.L. at the northern end of the town commanding the fork. The enemy may attack in any strength from any direction.

2. OWN TROOPS

The Senior Military Representative has at his disposal the following troops:-

Four Platoons, 3rd Herts Home Guard
Total effective strength - 180 (all ranks)

No. 1 Platoon Railway Home Guard
Effective strength - 36 (all ranks)

Detachment of North. Met. Elec. Power Co.
Effective strength - 20 men

TOTAL: 236 men

3. ARMS AND AMMUNITION

Weapon	No.	Ammo. available
Rifles .300	235	90 r.p.g.
Browning L.A.	5	400 r.p.g.
Browning M.G.	2	1000 r.p.g.
Northovers	4	
Spigot Mortars	Not yet issued	
Bombs	468 (This represents the entire Company stock)	

4. INTENTION

The enemy shall not be allowed to occupy the town of Stevenage, nor use the roads passing through the town. These shall be kept open for use of our own troops.

5. METHOD

On "Action Stations" the following positions will be taken-up and defended to the last man and the last cartridge.

GARRISON

KEEP (D.L. No. 1)	75 MEN No. 7 PLATOON AND 2 SECTORS OF No. 6
D.L. No. 2	20 MEN AND 2 SECTORS OF No. 6
D.L. No. 3 (Railway Platoon No. 8)	45 MEN No. 5 PLATOON
MOBILE RESERVE	40 MEN No. 1 PLATOON

KEEP (D.L. No. 1)

Situated at the southern end of the town on the High Street, Letchmore Road, Sish Lane, Trinity Road junction, this site closes all traffic through Stevenage from whatever quarter.

D.L. No. 2

Will be situated at the northern end of the High Street commanding the Hitchin and Baldock roads.

D.L. No. 3 - E.S.A. FACTORY

This factory is on Government Work; possesses its own Platoon of Herts Home Guard, and will be protected from all directions.

This factory D.L. will comprise a self-contained unit.

MOBILE RESERVE

No. 1 Platoon has for the past 2 years been training as a Mobile Platoon and will therefore retain the role of Mobile Reserve.

The Mobile Reserve will be based on the Keep and will be responsible for patrolling the following areas:-

NORTH TO JACKS HILL GARAGE
EAST - PIN GREEN AREA
SOUTH - CONTACT WITH KNEBWORTH
WEST - SYMONDS GREEN NORTON GREEN AREA

6. CONCEALMENT

The Spigot Mortars which it is proposed to site in D.L. No. 2, will require camouflaged concrete enplacements on the wide verge at the north end of the High Street.

The remaining D.L.'s afford no difficulties as walls of gardens and buildings are such as to render concealment an easy matter.

7. ROAD BLOCKS

No road blocks other than 'dannert' wire exist in Stevenage, and owing to the straightness of the road, it is not possible to site a block other than in an obvious position, which would be visible to the enemy at 700 yards. It is suggested that an abundance of A/T Mines be issued to the Garrison and that a 'Booby Trap' type of block should be used instead of the more conventional method.

Many small side streets are available in which mined boards might be concealed and drawn across the road in front of approaching A.F.V's.

It is suggested that near the Keep, a dummy road block of some dimensions might be sighted, so as to cause the enemy to halt, and afford the Garrison a 'sitting shot'.

8. **ADMINISTRATION**

(a) **Ammunition Supply**

On the man .... 50 rounds
Held in D.L. Reserve .... 30 rounds per man
Held in Central Reserve at Keep .... 10 rounds per man

(b) **Rations**

48 hour packs held in Headquarters, and 5 day rations in hand and earmarked for Home Guard Garrison.

(c) **Water**

Main supply from 2 Pumping Stations. Static water reserve of 1 gallon per man per day for 5 days arranged in D.L's.

(d) **Medical**

First Aid Pack in D.L's Central First Aid Post, 100 yards south of D.L. No. 2.

(e) **Decontamination**

27 High Street.

(f) **Blankets**

1 per 3 men.

(g) **Reserve Clothing**

5% Denim.

9. **PETROL AND FACTORY DEMOBILIZATION**

As per existing scheme vide "Standing Orders".

10. **INTERCOM**

Telephone to D.L's, then runners.

Mobile Reserve by cyclist or by quickest available method.

NOTE: A report issued at about the same time as the Defence Plan, stated that the following stores were required for adequate defence of Stevenage:

1000 S.I.P. Bombs, 700 Grenades No. 36, 400 Grenades No. 68, 200 Grenades No. 73, 2 Spigot Mortars, 4 0.300 L.M.G's (A.A. Mounting) 2000 R.P.G. for L.M.G's, 500 R.P.G. 0.455 for T.S.M.G's, and 400 A/T Mines.

The Home Guard gun pit in the High Street adjacent to the Two Diamonds and facing Orchard Road. The weapon on the left is a Spigot Mortar. A similar Spigot Mortar gun pit was sited near the Home Guard Headquarters. This photograph was taken during the invasion exercise held in 1942.
(The Pictorial)

APRIL, 1942

The Council granted permission for a 10,000 gallon static water tank to be erected on Bowling Green. This water is intended as an emergency supply for fire fighting. The Council also received a letter of complaint from the Rev. Hicks, regarding the habit of leaving bicycles unlocked outside A.R.P. premises and therefore of possible use to the enemy.

The following notice appeared in the Hertfordshire Pictorial, dated April 7th:

"YOUR JOB IF THE INVADER COMES. A SIMPLE EXPLANATION OF 84AA.

If the Germans invade, you will be wanting to lend a helping hand to the troops in throwing them back.

But your efforts, however willing, cannot be effective unless they are properly directed, and everybody else is taking his share. That is why regulation 84AA has come into being.

What does it mean? It means that the Regional Commissioner can declare the Region, or any part of it, to be an Operational Area. This gives the Ministry of Labour power to direct anyone in that area to carry out certain duties.

It might be just an ordinary useful job of work cutting a trench or building a defence post, or it might be a job for the naval, army or air force authorities; for a Government department or your local authority, or some public utility undertaking.

You will be paid for your job at the usual rates. If you are injured at work you will be compensated.

Members of the armed forces, the police, whole time civil defence, fire service, Observer Corps, and women's auxiliary services have their own jobs to do and are therefore exempt from the Order. You can only be asked to do work which appears to a competent military authority to be needed in connection with operations for meeting the enemy on land. You cannot be ordered under this regulation to do combatant duties.

Anyone refusing to comply with an order under this regulation can be sent to prison for not more than ten years or fined up a maximum of £500, or both."

The men of No. 6 Platoon Stevenage Home Guard have formed a 12 piece drum and bugle band. One of the platoon members, Pte. W. Cherry, is the bandmaster.

An advertisement in local newspapers states that from Monday, 27th April, a full meal comprising a meat pie, two vegetables and a pudding will be available for agricultural workers at a cost of 7d each. The advertisement, placed by the Hertfordshire War Agricultural Executive Committee, also lists a number of centres where the meal can be obtained and includes the Orchard Restaurant, Stevenage. The Committee have also introduced a 'pie scheme' to provide an extra meal for agricultural workers, which can be eaten at home or in the field. The pies can be bought by the workers (or their wives) between 8.30 am and 3 pm.

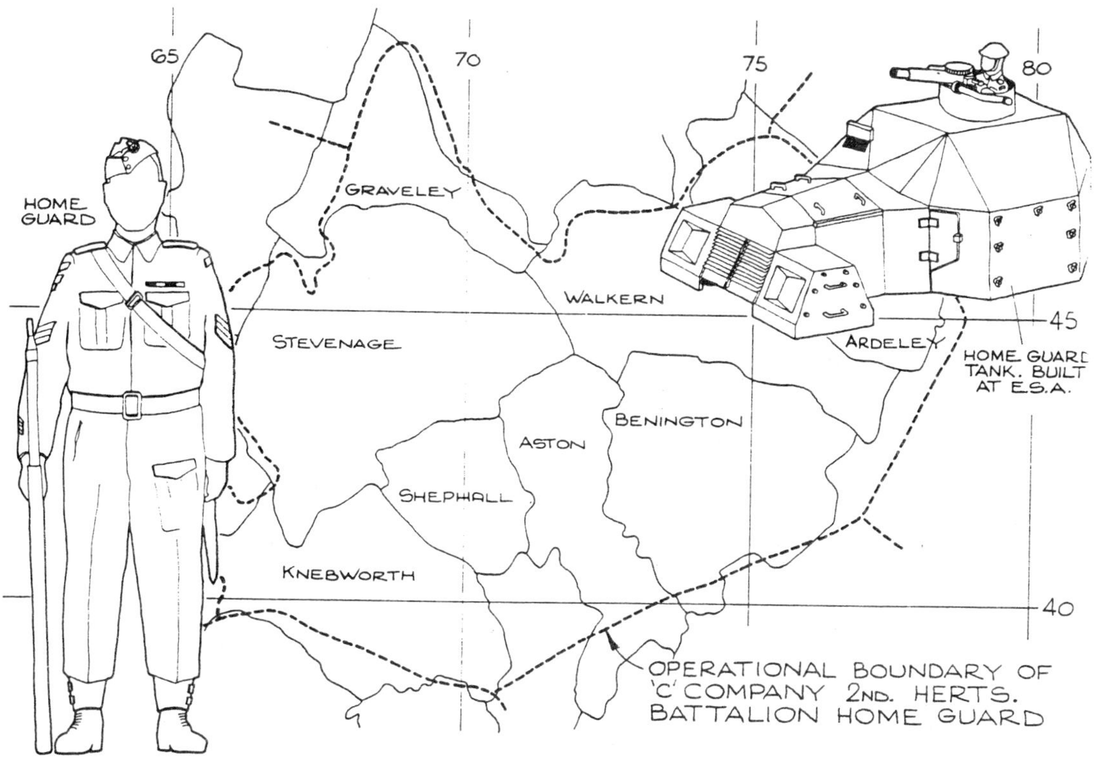

MAY, 1942

Headed by an R.A.F. band, approximately 150 local women war workers including many from Stevenage, marched from Hitchin Market Place to Messrs. Chalkleys Garage, Brand Street. The salute was taken by Air

Vice-Marshall MacEwen. The parade and a Women at Work exhibition at Chalkleys Garage is part of the general campaign to attract more women into the factories.

A branch of the newly formed Girls' Training Corps has been established in Stevenage. Mrs. C.H. Martin has been appointed Commandant, with Mrs. A.H. Horsfield as Quartermaster, Mrs. E. Bryceson as Adjutant, and Miss Ellis and Miss Brockett as Section Officers. The first parade of members has been arranged for Wednesday 3rd June at 8 pm in the Parish Rooms, Basils Road.

NOTE: The National Association of Girls' Training Corps was formed to provide pre-service training for girls aged between 16 and 18, on similar lines to the Air Training Corps. The cadets are given training in: despatch carrying, drill, fire fighting, anti-gas techniques, first aid, handywoman's course, hygiene, and physical training. The uniform comprises a white blouse, a navy skirt, and a navy beret with cap badge. The Stevenage group is registered as 346th G.T.C.

Stevenage Fire Guard training on Bury Mead. May 1942.
(The Pictorial)

At a recent W.V.S. progress meeting held in the Town Hall, it was reported that: the Old Castle Canteen had served 158,514 visitors since it was opened on 25th August 1940; garments made by the working party during 1941 amount to 672 pairs of socks, 21 pairs of sea boot stockings, 135 pairs of gloves, 107 woollen helmets, 23 jerseys and 43 scarves. The Orchard Restaurant, which is staffed by some W.V.S. volunteers, is serving approx. 400 people per day. An appeal was also made for more volunteers to help with the evacuee children billeted at The Grange.

National Savings for week ending 16th May amount to £3316. Regular house-to-house collections are being made in aid of the Red Cross and St. John Ambulance Joint War Organisation Penny-a-Week fund.

NOTE: The Penny-a-Week fund was launched in November 1939, and was designed to allow wage earners to contribute to the fund by direct deduction from wages. The scheme was extended in 1940 to include house-to-house collections.

An exhibition of boxing and unarmed combat held on the town football ground on Wednesday evening 27th May, was arranged by the 6th Company 3rd Battalion Herts. Home Guard. Proceeds were in aid of the Beds. and Herts. Regimental Prisoners of War Fund.

JUNE, 1942

A unit of the Stevenage National Fire Service was sent to assist at the fires caused by the recent air raids on Norwich.

The Council report that over 200 stirrup pumps have been supplied to Stevenage householders.

On Sunday, 28th June, Stevenage was subjected to a mock enemy attack to test the town's invasion preparations. All church services other than the 8 am were cancelled and the townsfolk were requested to stay indoors unless directly involved. The attack began with an 'enemy raid' at 10 am, which resulted in the High Street being littered with 'debris and casualties'. A number of 'fires' were started. The railway line by

A High Street scene during the invasion exercise held in the town on the 28th June, 1942. Note the debris caused by 'bombing', and the attacking 'enemy' aircraft. Also note the criss-cross pattern of the tape stuck on some shop windows. This was to reduce the danger of flying glass caused by bomb blast. (The Pictorial)

Trinity Road was blocked, and the Wardens Post at the junction of Fairview Road and Bridge Road was destroyed. The town's emergency services were called into action but were seriously hampered by persistent attacks from an 'enemy' fighter aircraft 'machine-gunning' the High Street. The Report and Control Centre telephone network was put out of action by a 'bomb' which fell on the building next door, and communication with the emergency services had to be maintained by the Messengers. (It was later reported that the failure of the telephone system was the cause of most of the problems experienced during the exercise). Some 60 people were evacuated from houses in Middle Row due to a large 'fire' and were given temporary shelter in the town Rest Centres. A further 'bombing' raid 'destroyed' the Lyric Hall in Orchard Road, the town's Post Office and Telephone Exchange, a house in Walkern Road, and one in Basils Road. The First Aid Post was soon crowded with 'casualties' and it was necessary to establish an emergency hospital in the Town Hall. A police car then toured the streets warning that an attack by 'enemy' troops was imminent and requesting List 2 men to report. The police also directed emergency service drivers to remove their vehicles from the roads as quickly as possible, to allow free movement of defending troops. The 'enemy' forces came into the town via Sish Lane and promply captured the Home Guard H.Q. and Keep (Stevenage Motor Co.), but were prevented from further progress by Home Guard positioned on the roofs of surrounding buildings. A force of regular troops arrived using Bren gun carriers, and cleared the town of the 'enemy' invaders.

The Fire Guard Service requested that some members of the Home Guard be released for fire guard duties.

JULY, 1942

The Council are to approach the Ministry of Production, regarding the provision of accommodation huts for war workers.

NOTE: Most of the factories in Stevenage are contracted to manufacture munitions. For example, both the Educational Supply Association Limited and the Vincent H.R.D. Motor Cycle Co. make parts for Mosquito aircraft. E.S.A. using their expertise in the manufacture of wooden structures are making parts of the aircraft wing, and Vincent H.R.D. manufacture small precision components. As the younger male workers are called to join the forces, they are replaced by women factory workers.

The following advertisement appears regularly in local newspapers.

> "URGENTLY REQUIRED - WOMEN WORKERS - FULL TIME OR PART TIME ON MUNITIONS - NO AGE LIMITS - GOOD WAGES AND CONDITIONS - DAY NURSERIES AND PLAY CENTRES FOR CHILDREN NOW BEING ARRANGED. APPLY:- MINISTRY OF LABOUR AND NATIONAL SERVICE, 10 EASTCHEAP, LETCHWORTH."

Many of the women are recruited from outside the town, and include some from as far away as Ireland. Most of the factories have instituted night shifts to meet the demanding production requirements. The E.S.A., Messrs. French & Son, Vincent H.R.D. Motor Cycle Co., and Messrs. George W. King, were established in the town before 1939. A. Ibbetson & Co. (Industrial Chemists) moved to Stevenage in 1941 when their factory in London was bombed, and W.H. Sanders (Electronics) Ltd. began in 1941 in a cowshed in Bedwell Lane.

SEPTEMBER, 1942

Permission has been granted for sheep to be grazed on Stevenage Cricket Ground during the winter months.

Arrangements have been made for all Fire Guard helmets to be lettered 'FG', at a cost of 1/- per dozen.

The emergency mortuary is to be moved from the Gas Works in Sish Lane to the premises of Shelford & Crowe in the High Street.

OCTOBER, 1942

Sch. Log, Oct. 5th-9th, "School closed for potato harvest."

A town salvage campaign is to be arranged which will include stalls in the High Street (staffed by the W.V.S.) for the collection of scrap metal.

Sch. Log, Oct. 12th, "School opened. Few farmers have so far harvested their potatoes. Requests received for labour. Farmers advised to try 'Land Girls Organisation' at Walkern, and the Military."

The management of the Orchard Restaurant, report that during the first year of operation, the restaurant served 105,101 meals.

Sch. Log, Oct. 19th, "During the Heads absence, a representative of the Ministry of Agriculture visited the school and implored Mr. Clarke to do his best to assist local farmers to lift both potatoes and beet crops. Twenty new boys were given permission to work in addition to those already employed."

Members of the Girls' Training Corps are currently assisting the local Home Guard Company with clerical duties.

Sch. Log, Oct. 21st, "The many boys working in the potato fields were caught in the rain and saturated: although no work was done, they were too wet to return to school."

Sch. Log, Oct. 27th, "Most boys returned to school: ground too wet."

NOVEMBER, 1942

The Council Highways and Lighting Committee have been notified that the fence protecting the Home Guard gun site on the west side of the High Street is damaged.

Sch. Log, Nov. 9th-10th, "Half term holiday. An effort was made to get all the senior boys on the land on both days."

Sch. Log, Nov. 16th, "Many boys still at work in the potato fields. Demands were made for many additional boys but none were available. Wear and tear of boots appears to be the reason for many not wishing to go."

Civil Defence Day was celebrated throughout the country on Sunday, 15th November. A parade of Stevenage units marched to St. Nicholas Church for a short service. The parade included: the Home Guard Band, the Police, Girls' Training Corps, Fire Guard, Air Training Corps, Ambulance Service, and National Fire Service.

DECEMBER, 1942

Re. The Clearance of Lofts Act 1940. The Council report that they have still not complied with the requirement to appoint an inspector.

Members of the Home Guard are being trained in fire fighting techniques by the town Fire Guard Service.

The practice of manning the Wardens Posts full time is to be discontinued until further notice. The wardens of Sector A5 are to donate their October subsistence allowance to the Red Cross Prisoners-of-War Fund.

A public display of fire fighting technique was presented by Fire Guard teams on Bury Mead field during the afternoon of Sunday 13th. A commentary on the action was given as the first team used a stirrup pump to deal with an incendiary bomb. Then a dummy house was set on fire by an incendiary bomb designed to explode some time after ignition. The Fire Guard controlled the house fire and (following the explosion), demonstrated the rescue of two casualties from the blaze. Wardens, First Aid Parties, Messengers (including several Girls' Training Corps members), and the Ambulance Service were also involved.

JANUARY, 1943

The management of Woolworths store in the High Street have requested that 12 of their staff be trained in fire fighting techniques.

Due to the recent increase in air raids, the town Wardens Posts are to be manned full time from January 20th.

FEBRUARY, 1943

Arrangements were made for the Girls' Training Corps to hold a social gathering at the Town Hall.

A War Agricultural Sub-Committee are trying to persuade the Council to convert a field near Ditchmore into allotments, but the Council Clerk has been directed to inform the Committee that a footpath crosses the field and also that it is the only place left to graze the Council horse.

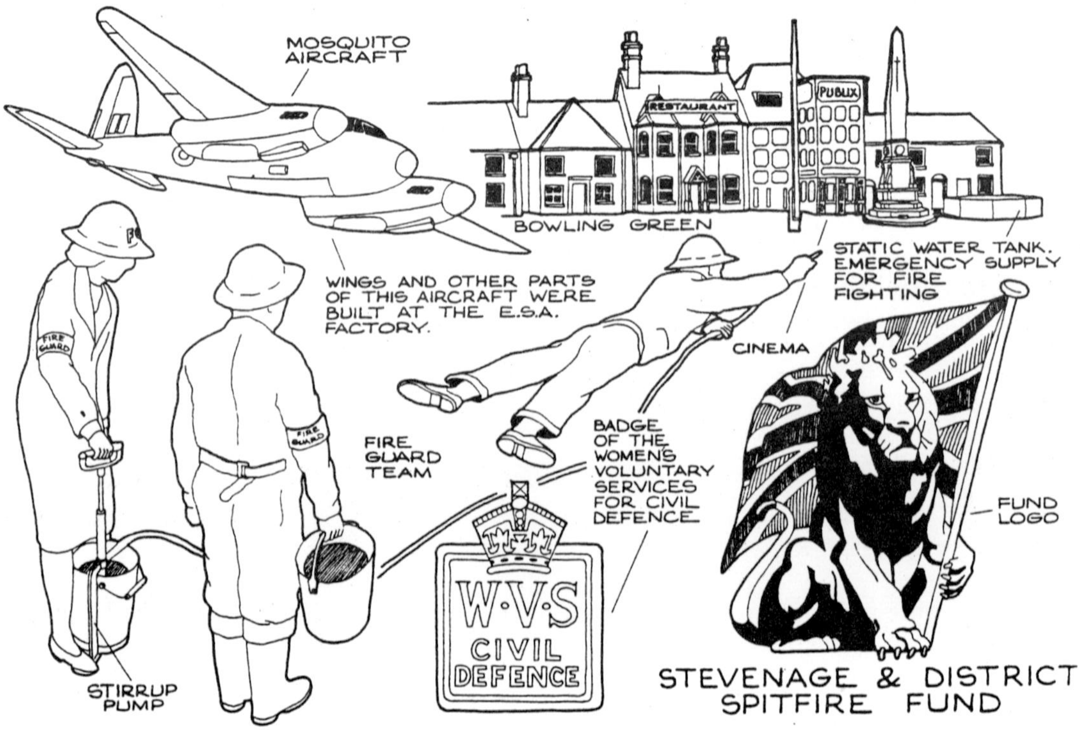

The Ministry of Home Security directed all Civil Defence authorities, to amalgamate the Rescue & First Aid Party Service into one unit to be known as the Civil Defence Rescue Service. The new amalgamated party is to consist of seven men including the driver. The Stevenage establishment is to be two parties.

MARCH, 1943

The Council are to issue Salvage Steward badges to voluntary workers who are engaged on this task.

The Fire Guard Staff Officer has been authorised to purchase forage-caps for the trailer pump crew at a cost of 8/6 each. (Due to the difficulty of obtaining the authorised service berets).

The Council granted permission for an additional static water tank to be erected adjacent to 65 High Street.

Re. The Clearance of Lofts Act 1940. The Council report that an inspection of 55 buildings has been completed, and that the occupiers of 16 premises were warned to clear their lofts or attics of inflammable material.

The Home Guard are to erect three Elephant Shelters on the Stevenage cricket ground, subject to the approval of the structures by the Council Surveyor and on the understanding that they are removed at the end of the war.

APRIL, 1943

On Tuesday, April 13th, an evening fire drill exercise was held at The Grange where approximately 80 evacuee boys are billeted. The A.R.P. services were alerted and teams of boys using stirrup pumps assisted the Fire Guard tackle several incendiary bombs. Twelve casualties were dealt with by the First Aid and Ambulance services. Mr. F.A. Millard J.P. & Chairman of Hitchin U.D.C., a visitor to The Grange, volunteered to act as a casualty and was lowered from a window on a stretcher. Some boys practiced escape drill using ladders placed against the building.

MAY, 1943

On Saturday the 8th, Commander Oliver Locker Lampson C.M.G., D.S.O., M.P., presented the town with a plaque to commemorate the adoption of H.M.S. Deodar.

Before the presentation was made, the Commander inspected a parade of the town Civil Defence Services including the Home Guard, Rescue & Decontamination Squads, Girls' Training Corps, Red Cross, St. John Ambulance Brigade, Air Training Corps, Boys' Brigade, Girl Guides, and A.R.P. Wardens. The event was organised by the Stevenage, Knebworth and District National Savings Committee, in conjunction with the Commissioners of the Admiralty. The parade was held in the grounds of Alleyne's Grammar School.

NOTE: H.M.S. DEODAR (T.124), adopted by the town during 1941, is a minesweeper trawler of 505 tons. Built at Goole in 1940, she is 150 ft × 17½ ft., and armed with one 12-pounder. In addition to the plaque, the ship's company presented the Town Council with a watercolour painting of the ship.

The town Holidays at Home Week is to be held this year from 31st July to 9th August. A Council sub-committee has written to the following organisations asking them to attend a meeting on Thursday, 3rd June, to determine what activities are to be provided during the week:-

E.S.A. Dramatic Society
The Amalgamated Engineering Union
The Chamber of Trade
The Cricket Club
Stevenage Football Club
The Carlton Lawn Tennis Club
Alleyne's Grammar School
County Council School
Church of England School
Youth Movement
Home Guard
St. John Ambulance
British Red Cross
National Fire Service
Air Training Corps
Girls' Traning Corps
The Bowling Club

The Council decided to have badges made for members of the newly formed Good Neighbour service. It is suggested that the badges should be plastic, about the size of a half crown, and have the name of the service printed on the face. It was also reported that some 30 qualified members of the Good Neighbour service have been issued with printed cards.

NOTE: During the autumn of 1938, a few W.V.S. branches began to give A.R.P. training to housewives who could not otherwise join a regular civil defence service, but would inevitably be involved in any emergency incident in their neighbourhood. The scheme has spread throughout the country and developed to include numerous other duties. Trained volunteers display a window card to indicate membership.

The town Invasion Committee met for the first time since 6th November 1942, and reported that only minor amendments regarding emergency food supplies are required to the town Civil Invasion Plan. The Committee have been directed to stay in being until further notice, but not to spend any more time or money.

Bren gun carriers belonging to the regular army assisting the Home Guard to clear the town of 'enemy' forces. This photograph, taken during the invasion exercise held in 1942, is looking towards the junction of Sish Lane with the High Street, and shows the front of the Sish Lane Methodist Church. (The Pictorial)

A target of £70,000 was set by the organisers of the local Wings for Victory Week which began on Saturday 22nd. Stevenage aimed to raise £50,000, the cost of ten Typhoons; and Knebworth £20,000, the cost of one Mosquito. Fund raising events began with a "Wings for Victory" Ball at the Town Hall on Wednesday 19th. Over 150 dancers attended and music for dancing was provided by an R.A.F. band. During the evening, four reproductions of "The Briefing" were presented by artist Frank Salisbury for auction in aid of the R.A.F. Benevolent Fund. The Week was officially opened on Saturday 22nd with an inter-services boxing tournament at the football ground. Following several bouts, a pair of football boots, autographed by members of the Arsenal Football Club, were auctioned.

Also during Saturday, the town watched an aerobatics display by a Mosquito flown by Geoffrey de Havilland. On Sunday an R.A.F. band led a parade to the Astonia Cinema via Letchmore Road, Walkern Road and the High Street. The parade included contingents of the R.A.F., W.A.A.F., N.F.S., A.T.S., Red Cross, Girl Guides, Land Army, Boys' Brigade, Civil Defence Services and Home Guard. The Home Guard and Letchworth A.T.C. also provided bands. At the Astonia a united service was conducted by the town clergy. In addition to dancing, evening events at the Town Hall included the shows: "It All Depends ....?" presented by the E.S.A. Concert Party, a "Wings for Victory" revue by sixty boys and girls of the R.A.F., and "Black and Amber" by the concert party of "G" Division Metropolitan Police.

NOTE: Stevenage raised £67,240.

Sch. Log, May 28th, "The school saved £272-8-0 during the Wings for Victory Week. The target was £200. £60 was invested from the school gardening account."

Part of a parade in support of the local 'Wings for Victory Week' National Savings Campaign, held during May 1943. The photograph shows "C" Company Home Guard led by the Company band, just passing Basil's Road. (The Pictorial)

JUNE, 1943

The Fire Guard Service purchased 50 whistles at a cost of £3, for issue to newly enrolled fire guards.

A nursery has opened in Sish Lane, with places for 35 children aged between 2 and 5 years, (H.C.C. Wartime Nursery).

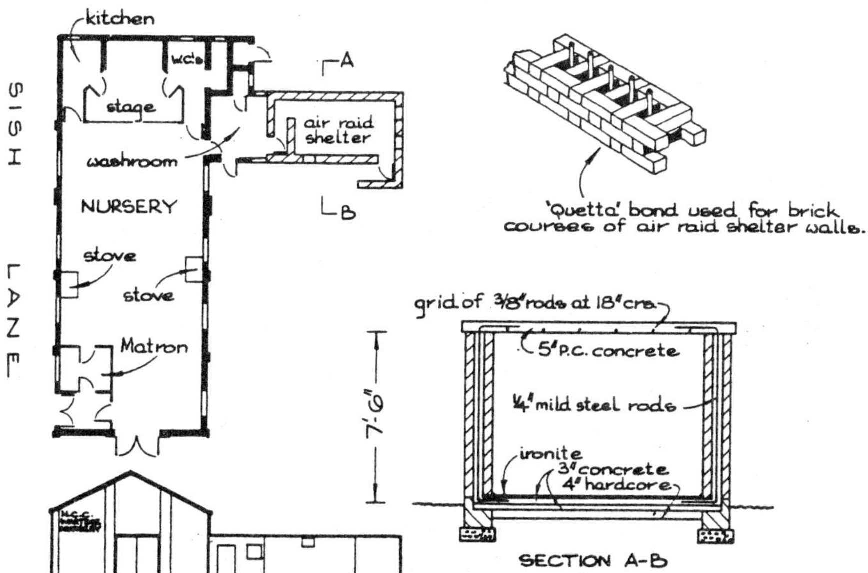

HERTS. COUNTY COUNCIL
WARTIME NURSERY SISH LANE.

JULY, 1943

The town Finance and Rating Committee report that the current financial state of the forthcoming Workers Holidays at Home Week, is: expenses £304-10-0, and receipts (not including donations) £229-0-0. A bank account is to be opened in the name of the Workers Holiday Committee.

The Council purchased two additional air raid warning sirens at a cost of £65.

50 persons completed their training for the town Good Neighbour service.

Sch. Log, July 9th, "Result of 'old iron' salvage drive; 3 tons 19 cwt (according to letter received from Mr. ... U.D.C. surveyor)."

AUGUST, 1943

Events held during the Workers Holidays at Home Week included: a children's fair on Whitesmead Recreation Ground; intertown cricket matches between Stevenage and Letchworth and Stevenage and Hitchin; a bowls tournament; open-air dancing; a fete with displays of flowers, vegetables, jams, arts, hobbies, etc; athletics; a boxing tournament and a treasure hunt. Whist drives, dances and a variety concert were held at the Town Hall. The last event of the week was a baseball match between two U.S. Army Air Force teams.

Mr. Marsden Popple, Chairman of the Stevenage Urban District Council, opening the local 'Workers Holidays at Home Week' on Saturday 31st July 1943. In the background is seen part of the fair held during that week on Whitesmead Recreation Ground.
(The Pictorial)

SEPTEMBER, 1943

The Royal Berkshire Regimental Band presented a concert on the Bowling Green on Tuesday, 31st August. On Monday, 6th September, they played at a garden party held at Springfield House in aid of the Hertfordshire Troops Welfare Fund. Invited guests at the party included wounded from a local hospital, members of the forces, and the Women's Land Army.

A limited version of the Stevenage Charter Fair was held in Pound Avenue from September 22nd until October 2nd. The fair opened early afternoon each day, and closed before black-out time.

The Home Guard held a concert and social at the Town Hall on the 18th September, and permission was granted for alcoholic drinks to be allowed on the premises.

A Battle of Britain parade comprising units of the local Civil Defence Services, was held on 26th September followed by a service in the Parish Church.

The Fire Guard Service issued the following up-dated list of Deputy Sector Captains:

Sector 102, Mr. S. Chambers, 3 Nottingham Road
Sector 103, Mr. H. Scott, 43 Green Street
Sector 104, Mr. E. Smith, 86 Fairview Road
Sector 105, Mr. Harper, 'Southsea', London Road
Sector 106, Mr. B.L. Newbury, Grove Road
Sector 107, Mr. A.E. Coulson, 44/46 Albert Street
Sector 108, Mr. B.H. Field, 7 Hellards Road
Sector 109, Mr. J.P. Walker, 8 Lawrence Avenue
Sector 110, Mr. C. Dymoke, 19 Church Lane

OCTOBER, 1943

It has been reported that the National Fire Service static water tank adjacent to 65 High Street, is leaking.

The local W.V.S. have adopted two prisoners of war, and are arranging to send them comforts in the form of cigarettes, clothing and books, etc.

The Welfare Committee are currently organising Sunday evening entertainment at the Town Hall for women war workers billeted in Stevenage. The Council are providing the Town Hall free of charge.

During a recent air raid when several bombs were dropped in the Shephall area, it is reported that many Stevenage people rushed from their homes to see what had happened. The Council warned that this was not only very dangerous but since several people left their doors open, the black-out regulations were contravened.

NOVEMBER, 1943

The following activities are to be held at the Town Hall during the next few weeks:-

1. Dance in aid of the Association of Friends of the French Volunteers.
2. Lecture on the 8th Army, in aid of the Red Cross.
3. Whist drive in aid of H.M.S. Deodar Comforts Fund.
4. Military band concert in aid of H.M.S. Deodar Comforts Fund.
5. Dance in aid of H.M.S. Deodar Comforts Fund.
6. Christmas Party for First Aid Post personnel.
7. Home Guard dance.
8. Dance for personnel of Prichard & Gold.

Nine Fire Guard Officers have been issued with greatcoats, battledress uniforms and boots.

A 'casualty' being assisted to the town First Aid Post during the invasion exercise held in 1942. The two ladies standing by the railings (which were later removed for salvage) are wearing Fire Guard helmets. (The Pictorial)

The night time manning level of the town Civil Defence Services is now as follows:-

The Report & Control Centre: one messenger and one whole time member Sunday to Friday. Three part time members Saturday nights.

Ambulance Depot: one driver, one attendant and one whole time member Sunday to Friday. Three part-time members Saturday nights.

First Aid Post: one whole time member and one part-time member, Sunday, Monday, Tuesday and Friday. Two part-time members, Wednesday and Saturday.

DECEMBER, 1943

Sch. Log, Dec. 1st, "Mr. ... H.M.I. called to go into the question of receiving 15 pupils from the L.C.C. school quartered in the Parish Rooms."

The Council bought an ambulance from Ealing County Council at a cost of £40. This is to replace the vehicle loaned to the Council by Mrs. Inns.

The next fortnightly meeting of the town A.R.P. Wardens (normally held at the Town Hall), is to be held in Alleyne's Grammar School when a speaker from London will talk on the 'Blitz'.

SOME UNIFORMED CIVIL DEFENCE WORKERS

FEBRUARY, 1944

Sch. Log, Feb. 3rd, "A collection for the Prisoners of War Fund realized £2.19.4. There was a balance of £1.6.11. The total of £4.6.3. has now been transferred to a special cash account."

A local Army Cadet Force unit is to be formed.

A complaint about the state of repair of the fence surrounding the Home Guard gun site on the east side of the High Street opposite Orchard Road, has been received by the Highways & Lighting Committee.

MARCH, 1944

The Council received numerous complaints about damage to the town caused by military vehicles. Damaged areas include Fairview Road.

APRIL, 1944

Funds raised during the year ending March 31st 1944 at the various events held in aid of the Red Cross and St. John Ambulance Joint War Organisation amount to just over £1800. House-to-house collections and the Penny-a-Week Fund raised £594, the Prisoners-of-War Fund collections £416, the Christmas Toy Fair £281, and the Gymkhana and Horticultural Show £280. The flag days and cinema collections added just over £229.

Of the 9000 books collected by Mr. Roach and a team of boys, some will be sent to the forces and some to war-damaged public libraries. The rest will go for salvage.

This photograph shows No. 40 Detachment of the British Red Cross Society, the nursing staff of the town First Aid Post. The male in the group is Dr. Skeggs, the post Medical Officer. c1941.

MAY, 1944

The Stevenage Civil Defence Ambulance Unit report that they now have four ambulances. One is owned by the Council, one by the County Council, and the rest are privately owned.

Organisers of the local Salute The Soldier Week to be held from the 13th to the 20th May, are hoping to improve on the sum collected during last years Wings for Victory Week and have set a target of £70,000. The programme of events to be held during the week includes the following:

a) A battle display by the R.E.M.E. and the local Home Guard.
b) A concert by the band of the Royal Artillery.
c) A show by the E.S.A. Concert Party.
d) A parade by local Civil Defence units, followed by a service at the Astonia cinema.
e) A "Salute The Soldier" dance at the Town Hall to music provided by the band of the Royal Horse Guards.
f) A presentation of the show "Quit Stalling" by the R.A.F. Riding High Revue Party.
g) Dancing displays by the pupils of the Joan Winchester School of Dancing.
h) An exhibition each evening by the local Home Guard.

JUNE, 1944

A hostel in the North Road has been taken over by the Workers Travel Association and is to be used for billeting 26 male Irish war workers.

The campaign to liberate Europe from enemy occupation began on June 6th when Allied invasion forces landed on the French coast at Normandy.

Sch. Log, June 14th, "Salute the Soldier (COLLECTION) result: £290.0.0, Target £250."

Sch. Log, June 27th, "School closed in the afternoon. Exhibition baseball match by the American Forces."

A Location Statement dated June 1944 and issued by the 2nd Battalion Hertfordshire Home Guard, indicates that the normal and battle H.Q. for 'C' Company is 146 High Street Stevenage, with the Coach & Horses Public House opposite as an emergency alternative.

NOTE: The H.Q. is referred to as the 'Keep' in the Stevenage Defence Scheme.

Other Location Statements issued at this time indicate that the following units come within 'C' Company operational area:

a) WAR OFFICE STAGING CAMP
MAJOR G.B. CARMICHELL
THE WARREN, STEVENAGE. TEL. 365

b) ES.6 WAR DEPARTMENT
LT. COL. R.J. BLISS R.E.
ASTON HOUSE, STEVENAGE. TEL. SHEPHALL 213

c) SIGNALS OFFICE, 9TH. ARM. DIV. SIGNALS
2ND. LT. J.D. RENNIE
BROADWATER HOUSE, STEVENAGE. TEL. KNEB. 3141

JULY, 1944

The new social club for women war workers was opened on Sat. 8th by Lady Bragg. The club building, which is sited in Pound Avenue and is to be known as the Lytton Club, was built by Messrs. Geo. W. King Ltd. The Ministry of Labour paid for the building, and a grant of £510 from an American Women's organisation provided most of the furniture, etc. Facilities at the club include: an entertainments hall, a kitchen and dining room, a laundry plus drying room with provision for ironing, and living quarters for the club warden.

AUGUST, 1944

Incident Message 23/09/44, 09.30, "Two Fortress's crashed at Weston – one in the Park and one in field opposite The Anchor P.H., Weston Road. 2 fatal casualties, woman and child." From: STEVENAGE POLICE.

Ambulances from Stevenage attended the crash at Weston.

Mr. Donald King of Geo. W. King Ltd., received the following letter from General Sir F.A. Pile, Bt., K.C.B., D.S.O., M.C., General Officer Commanding-in-Chief A.A. Command:-

Donald King Esq.,
Geo. W. King Ltd.,
Argyle Works,
Fairview Road,
Stevenage, Herts.

August, 1944

Dear Mr. King,

I have been informed by Brigadier Burls of the splendid efforts which you and your staff contributed toward the rapid preparation of defence measures in connection with the flying bomb attack.

In extending to you and your staff my personal thanks, and keen appreciation of all that has been done, may I assure you that we, on our part, will use the now completed apparatus to the best advantage, and that, in fact, we are already achieving a rising scale of successes against this nuisance.

Yours very sincerely,

F.A. PILE
GENERAL, G.O.C.-IN-C.
(ANTI-AIRCRAFT COMMAND)

NOTE: Soon after the start of the flying bomb attacks, it was decided to use all the available anti-aircraft guns to form a defensive barrier along the south coast. To aid rapid deployment of the guns, King's were asked to manufacture portable gun platforms. The platforms were constructed in sections, and within 2000 working hours of receiving the order, the Company had produced approximately 205,000 pieces.

SEPTEMBER, 1944

Incident Message 05/09/44 05.30, "2 Flys' passed over Stevenage falling at Leysgreen and Kings Walden respectively. No casualties. Slight damage to cottages. Some ceilings down at Stevenage. Windows broken at Hitchin." From: STEVENAGE POLICE.

Due to the temporary closing of the Bunyan Baptist Church as a Rest Centre, 69 High Street has been requisitioned for the accommodation of homeless persons.

The Council received a number of complaints about the over-enthusiastic use of whistles by Fire Guards.

OCTOBER, 1944

Sch. Log, Oct. 19th, "School closed for a week ...... half term holiday. 40 boys volunteered to work at potato picking."

Sch. Log, Oct. 23rd, "School opened after a week's holiday. Twenty boys potato picking for Mr. Moules."

NOVEMBER, 1944

The number of evacuees in the town is now 441.

The Home Guard were ordered to 'stand down' on the 1st November. A national Home Guard 'stand-down' parade has been arranged and will be held in Hyde Park London on the 3rd December, 1944.

DECEMBER, 1944

The three Companies of the 2nd Battalion Hertfordshire Home Guard (approx. 900 men), held a final parade on Sunday, 3rd December when they attended a farewell service at the Hermitage Cinema, Hitchin. The men of 'C' Company (Stevenage & District H.G.) paraded outside their H.Q. on the corner of Trinity Road before marching through the High Street to Stevenage Station, led by the Company band.

Listed below are the 'C' Company Officers and the location of Company premises at the time of 'stand-down':-

'C' Company H.Q., 146 High Street, Stevenage.
Company Officers: Major A.G. Howard
Capt. R.A.V. White M.C.
Capt. T.E. Tatham
Lieut. B.G. Ashman, Signals Officer
Lieut. S. Stutley, Intelligence Officer
Lieut. H.J. Bowen-Simpkins, Weapon Training Officer
2nd Lieut. J.W. Scrivens, Gas Officer
2nd Lieut. H.G. Little, Ammunition Officer

No. 21 Platoon, Rookery Yard, Stevenage.
Officers: Lieut. R.W. Madgin, 2nd Lieut. H.S. Kings

No. 22 Platoon, (?)
Officers: Lieut. W.C.W. Harris M.C., Lieut. F. Dowton

No. 23 Platoon, Old Rectory, Walkern
Officers: Lieut. C.W. Sworder, Lieut. T.J. Swain

No. 24 Platoon, Aston & Benington
Officers: Lieut. W. Barnes, Lieut. E.P.B. Baggallay

No. 25 Platoon, E.S.A. Factory, Stevenage.
Officers: Lieut. T.R. North, Lieut. J. Briars

No. 26 Platoon, 27 Hitchin Road, Stevenage.
Officers: Lieut. W.A. Bulleid, Lieut. J. Allen

No. 27 Platoon, E.S.A. Factory, Stevenage.
Officers: Lieut. J. Bowie, Lieut. W.D. Timms

No. 28 Platoon, Stevenage Motor Company, Stevenage.
Officers: Lieut. P.S. Kitchener, 2nd Lieut. A. Bennett

No. 29 Platoon, (?)
Officers: Lieut. A.G. Saunders, Lieut. E. Walker M.C.

No. 30 Platoon, The Village Hall, Ardeley
Officers: Lieut. T.C. Sutcliffe, Lieut. C.H. Boorman

No. 31 Platoon, (?)
Officers: Lieut. A.E. Nye, 2nd Lieut. F. Manning

Chapter 2

THE LAST FEW MONTHS: JANUARY-MAY 1945

With the Allied forces firmly established on the European mainland, 1945 began with almost universal belief that the end of the war was now within reach. The threat of invasion had finally disappeared and the Home Guard had been 'stood-down'. The Civil Defence Services were still in action however, dealing with the flying bomb and long range rocket attacks which had begun the previous June and were to continue until the end of March. (The last flying bomb to evade the defensive barrier fell at Datchworth just before 9 a.m. on 29th March.) Six of the town Rest Centres were closed in January, leaving just the Bunyan Baptist Hall and the Parish Hall in Basils Road fully staffed and equipped for any emergency. But from April on, all the remaining Civil Defence premises began to be closed and the organisations disbanded.

As the Allied forces liberated enemy-held territory, so the prisoners-of-war were released and returned home. One of the first Stevenage men to return was Pte. R. Nye of Walkern Road. He was met at Stevenage station by his parents plus friends and neighbours, and then escorted to his flag-decorated home for a celebration. The Council had recently established a fund for returning prisoners-of-war and one of the events planned by the fund committee was a celebration supper for the prisoners. When the town Fire Guard disbanded, they donated the balance of their general fund, £5-6s-8d, to the Council's fund for prisoners-of-war.

The war in Europe finally ended in May, and although the war against Japan continued until August, it had little influence on the rapid reduction of the Civil Defence Services. (VE Day was celebrated on 8th May and VJ Day on 15th August.)

Victory celebrations in various forms were held throughout the town during the spring and summer months. A Victory Parade was held on Sunday 13th May when units of the town's Civil Defence organisations assembled together for the last time. Led by the combined bands of the Home Guard and Army Cadets, the parade marched through the High Street to the Astonia Cinema to attend a short thanksgiving service conducted by Canon Morgan Smith. Throughout that same week, the Catholic Church and Rectory gardens in Basils Road, the Cromwell Hotel and the War Memorial, were floodlit. There were celebration bonfires at Fishers Green, Whitesmead Recreation Ground, Trinity Road and Longcroft Road; and a firework display in Pound Avenue. Several VE dances were held at the Lytton Club, and on one occasion it is reported that the dancers left the club and danced round the local streets. Also, approximately 30 members of the club, who must have been the last of the women war workers still billeted in the town, were invited one Sunday to a party given at the local U.S. 8th Air Force Camp. During the first week of July the E.S.A. Concert Party presented a revue at the Town Hall entitled "Victory Parade". Victory parties were held in several streets in the town including Walkern Road, Albert Street and Alleyns Road. In October, the Stevenage, Knebworth and District National Savings Committee held a Thanksgiving Savings Weeks with a target of £50,000, and asked householders to decorate their houses with flags and bunting, etc.

Many of the organisations held 'farewell parties' to celebrate the end of active service, but there can be little doubt that these events were also sad occasions. Whilst they were thankful that the war was over, the members recognized that they would miss the comradeship that comes from serving with such an organisation.

Of the 335 evacuees still billeted in the town at the end of the war, 237 returned home during June. By the end

A scene from the ESA Concert Party review entitled "Victory Parade", presented at the Town Hall in July 1945. (The Pictorial)

of July there were just 98 left; 30 at the Grange, 29 at Ballam Nursery, 9 at the Priory, 5 in requisitioned property and 25 with householders. By September this number had reduced to 60. A few evacuees decided to make Stevenage their home and remained to work and marry in the town.

The number of war workers still billeted in the town at the end of the war was 471.

Premises and sites which were still being used by the Civil Defence Service etc., and which the Council were now anxious to vacate as soon as possible, included the following:-

a) The First Aid Post at 27 High Street
b) The Ambulance Depot at 31 High Street
c) The Report & Control Centre at 9 Orchard Road
d) The A.R.P. store at 8 High Street
e) The A.R.P. Officer's office at The Council premises
f) The air raid shelter on Mrs. Chalkley's land in Church Lane
g) The brick static water tank on Bowling Green
h) The steel static water tank on Letchmore Green
i) The steel static water tank at the High Street end of Albert Street
j) The Home Guard hut in Trinity Road
k) The Wardens Post in Whitesmead Recreation Ground

Obviously in many cases the buildings and sites had to be cleared and returned to their original state. Permission to build wartime structures had generally only been granted on condition that they were removed at the end of the war. A few wartime structures were, however, converted to peace time use. The tenants of cottages in Ditchmore Lane asked the Council if they could buy the air raid shelters built on their land, and a well-designed shelter built by Mr. Briars in his garden in Whitesmead Road was converted into a useful store. The town air raid warning siren, mounted on a structure adjacent to the fire station in Basils Road and until now the responsibility of the Council, was handed over to the N.F.S. The front room of 14 Southsea Road, which had been used as a Wardens Post since the early days of the war, was redecorated by the Council before being returned to its original owner.

In spite of the run down of the Civil Defence organisations and the munitions industry, there was still a serious shortage of labour. The Council even requested permission to use Italian prisoners-of-war on town refuse collection. This request was refused, but many prisoners were employed on local farms until long after the war had ended. There was also a shortage of building materials and the Council erected several prefabricated temporary houses in Sish Lane. (Generally known as 'prefabs').

The First Aid Post closed in May. During its five and a half years of active service the post treated well over 200 casualties, and in addition to their duties at the post many of the members also worked in the local hospitals.

In June the Council wrote to the Showman's Guild stating their intention to resume the annual Charter Fair that coming September, but due to the volume of military traffic still using the Great North Road, they asked the Guild to consider holding the fair somewhere other than in the High Street.

As the women war workers billeted in Stevenage began to return home, so the need for the Lytton Club came to an end. By mid 1946 the use of the building had changed from a social club for women war workers, to a Community Centre (or Citizens Club as they were then called) for local families.

The Ambulance Service left the Club and Institute building at the end of July, although the Council kept the service running until the H.C.C. Ambulance Service was formed. The fact that the Stevenage Civil Defence Ambulance Service transported 238 cases to hospital during 1944, indicated its value to the local community.

Members of the Stevenage Civil Defence Ambulance Service, photographed in the grounds of Springfield House. The title Civil Defence superseded the earlier title of Air Raid Precautions. c1944.

The W.V.S., like all the other Civil Defence Services, was officially 'stood-down' at the end of the war, but this organisation had become such a valuable social welfare service that it remained in being. (One official history of wartime services lists over 140 separate activities for which the W.V.S. were directly responsible). The name of the organisation was changed for a third time when the suffix Civil Defence was deleted and it became simply the Women's Voluntary Services. The Stevenage unit moved their H.Q. from the Council offices in Orchard Road to 96 High Street, where they remained for some years.

The forces canteen was one of the last wartime services to be 'stood-down'. By the time the Old Castle Canteen finally closed its doors on 16th November, 1946, the volunteer staff had served 860,614 cups of tea, 102,076 main meals, 793,775 subsidiary meals and 50,100 minerals and cordials. All in just over six years.

During the time of the Normandy invasion there was a considerable increase in the volume of military traffic passing through Stevenage and since the town was a designated 'staging camp' many convoys stayed overnight. Although the movement of a convoy was in theory secret, the military authorities generally advised the canteen manager when a convoy could be expected. It was said by one canteen worker that in spite of the secrecy it was generally possible to arrange a dance at the Town Hall in time for the arrival of a convoy. During its busiest period, the canteen was open from 6.30 a.m. until the early hours of the following morning, and serving as many as two thousand customers per day.

One of the many street parties held in the town to celebrate victory. This one was in Alleyns Road. (Mr. & Mrs. Chance)

Little wonder that their slogan became, "Never have so many been served so quickly by so few".

The following letter giving notice of the intention to close the canteen, was sent to each member of the staff:-

THE OLD CASTLE CANTEEN
STEVENAGE
HERTFORDSHIRE

Date 5th November, 1946

Dear

It will probably be no surprise to you to learn that at last the Old Castle Canteen is to be closed on November 16th.

You know how well it has fulfilled its functions to the many thousands who passed through here since 1940, when on many occasions the work was extremely arduous, and also especially during the winter and spring before D-Day. It is no exaggeration to say that without your invaluable help and hard work, and that of others, it could not possibly have been the success it undoubtedly had been.

As you know I have had several letters from High Authority, and many from men in the Forces of appreciation and thanks for the work you have done for the Services. I feel that in sending you this notice, I would ask you to accept my heartfelt thanks for the marvellous support you have given to me personally in all those long and difficult years. To me, the feeling of regret at the finish of our work together is compensated by the friendship and comradeship that has grown between us in our joint effort.

Good Luck and thank you

Yours sincerely,

(sd.) Helen Inns.

PLUS THE FOLLOWING HAND WRITTEN NOTE ON SOME LETTERS:

"Also for your untiring work in knitting comforts for local members of the Forces".

Volunteer staff of The Old Castle Canteen. The canvas sheet is covered with military badges presented to the canteen by visiting servicemen. C1945

At a farewell dinner given by the staff in honour of Mrs. Helen Inns, who had managed the Old Castle Canteen since it opened, many visitors praised the work of the canteen. During the six years it was open, the canteen had always provided a friendly atmosphere for visiting service personnel and hundreds of letters of appreciation were received from servicemen all over the world. Also on display at the dinner, was a large canvas covered with badges and insignia given to the canteen by visiting servicemen. The variety of badges testified to the many nationalities and services that had used the canteen.

The menu for the dinner, which was held at the Town Hall on 18th December, gives an insight into the difficulty at that time of predicting what foods would be available at any particular time. The printed menu was limited to predicting that the meal would include 'thick soup' and 'hot roast meat'. Even the sweet course was changed at the last minute from apple pie to fruit salad.

Members of all the organisations received letters from several official sources including locally the Stevenage Urban District Council, thanking them for their services. Most of the members also qualified for the 1939– 45 Defence Medal.

Considering all that had happened during the six years of war, it is surprising just how little interest was shown in its ending. The victory celebrations and the disbanding of the various organisations described above, generally commanded little more than a brief report on the inside pages of local newspapers. After all the effort involved in forming and training the Civil Defence units, plus the many hours of active duty undertaken by the members, it is hard to accept that this national service should be rewarded with so little public acclaim. But perhaps the local newspapers correctly reflected the mood of the people at the end of the war. They were tired of the war, and in spite of the food rationing and many other hardships that still existed, the people were thankful that the threat to national freedom had passed. The war could now be quietly forgotten and they could return to their normal peaceful way of life. Sadly, for the 37 families of those men who lost their lives in the defence of that freedom, life could never completely return to normal.

"War should belong to the tragic past, to history; it should find no place on humanity's agenda for the future."

Pope John Paul II, Coventry 1982

Chapter 3

"I SHALL ALWAYS REMEMBER ...."

The following personal memories of wartime Stevenage are short extracts from some of the interviews held with the townspeople listed in Section 2.

STEVENAGE URBAN DISTRICT COUNCIL

"Mr. W.T. Workman (Head of Alleyne's Grammar School at that time), ... gave considerable service during the early part of the A.R.P. He and I (Mr. P.T. Ireton) were commissioned by the Council to draw up an organisation for the Stevenage A.R.P. as it was then called."

"Mr. Marsden Popple, who was Chairman of the Stevenage Urban District Council from 1939 to 1945, gave outstanding service to the town. He gave up his activities in the city to devote his whole time to the local war effort. He also acted as Chief Warden .... "

REPORT AND CONTROL CENTRE

"The Report and Control Centre was in Orchard Road, in the annexe to the Old Town Hall and in what was the Rating Evaluation Office. It was protected by sandbags and concrete, and was manned initially by volunteers but later we had 3 people full-time on an eight hour rota. We had bunks so that we could sleep there and the volunteers manned the Centre at weekends."

"When war broke out, we were using a warning system where we were given preliminary warnings. As Officer-in-Charge, I would get what they called a 'purple', which was the preliminary warning. I then rushed on my bicycle down to the Control Centre, only to be told when I arrived that they had got the 'white'; so I would go home again. And often when I got home, my wife would tell me that we had got another 'purple', so I would have to turn the bike round and go back again. And so it went on until the Government changed the system."

"The 1st Stevenage Scout Troop provided messenger boys from the eldest lads and they covered the Report and Control Centre and the Police Station in Stanmore Road. You slept overnight at the Report and Control Centre on a voluntary rota basis. A full-time officer was in charge, a Mr. Cannon, also another volunteer officer I remember, Bebe Gibbons. We had refreshments, coffee made with dried milk and mulligatawny soup. To read, there was a supply of the American Geographical Magazine handed in by Mr. Popple, then Chairman of the Council. There were few incidents that I remember but Mr. Cannon had a great thing going about his operations, particularly of the stomach and his dice with death in the dubious care of hospitals. The time spent was from 10 at night until 7 in the morning. You slept on a bunk bed made up with rough army blankets and wearing your Scout's uniform."

FIRST AID POST

"We had a rota all throughout the day ... I usually did night duty ... we slept there (at the First Aid Post), but we got up when the siren went ... we had to get up and fill the hot water bottles; well that was the plan, but it was always a good excuse to have a cup of tea .... There was always somebody on duty at the telephone; mostly it was Mrs. Richardson or Dorothy Grosvenor ... On the right-hand side was the room where the telephone was, and then we eventually made that into a surgery, all set out with instruments and things ... we did quite a few minor operations ... it had to be kept in readiness and absolutely clean. Mrs. White, our Commandant, was very strict indeed; she was a marvellous Commandant. At the back was a kitchen .... We slept in the room upstairs where we had beds and masses of blankets. We all did some sort of hospital duty as well ... as part of our training."

AMBULANCE SERVICE

"All these things were Government sponsored, and every town had to have an ambulance service for A.R.P., and so it was through the Council that it was organised. Mr. Slow, who gave a lot of the local A.R.P. lectures, was asked to become head of the Ambulance Depot. We had one ambulance that came through the Council, and then we had our own private cars. Later we had two permanent ambulances, and two full-time workers."

"We had first aid classes in the Town Hall given by a Mr. Greenwood ...... we did our training on an E.S.A. furniture van. Although we did not have many bombs around here, the Ambulance Service was quite busy ... taking people to hospital. I twice got called out (I was an ambulance driver), once to pick up a serviceman who had walked out of a train between the two Welwyn tunnels, and another one who somehow got out of a train at Langley Sidings. We were once called out to somewhere near Weston, where it was thought that a 'plane had come down' ... I think we had two ambulances ... one which was called Little Audrey..."

"We used to sleep down at the depot .... We started off by just having it manned by two people, and whenever we got a 'yellow' warning, we were 'phoned' and had to get up and drive down to the depot (often in the middle of the night) and that got a bit wearing especially as we all had daytime jobs too ... eventually we had a rota ... you were either on from 8 to midnight, or midnight to 8 next morning. Generally, people who had jobs were on from 8 to midnight, perhaps once or twice a week, and then at the weekend they did their night shift ... Some of the St. John's Ambulance people were with us and they acted as ambulance attendants if we had to go out on an incident."

"We also had 'sitting cars' for people who were capable of sitting and didn't have to be carried on a stretcher ... we took them to hospital ... Hitchin or Queen Victoria at Old Welwyn ..... we even took expectant mothers occasionally ... the team was one driver, one attendant and perhaps a St. John's man ..."

"I remember all our ambulances were called out to go to Potters Bar once ... to pick up a train load of soldiers from France ... after D-Day."

FIRE SERVICE

"Our first pump was, I should think, about 250 gallons-per-minute ... ; a light pump ... It was towed (at first) by local tradesman, coal merchants, etc. ... We used to man the Fire Station continually (5 men to a team) ... We used to hitch the pumps, and at the warning we used to start off round Stevenage. Now this didn't last long because I can only ever remember going about once ... so if anything happened, within ten minutes ... pumps could converge on the incident ... Then they started buying old motor cars ... we had a big American one ... that was the early part of the war ... Then we had A.T.V's, Austin Towing Vehicles, which were made and equipped for the job. We used to tow the pump behind it. The inside of the body, we used to put all the equipment for firemen (and) perhaps your blankets, iron rations, etc .... We used to go out on 'regional calls' and we went to Norwich when they had those 'Baedeker' raids, and there were, it seemed, hundreds of these Austin Towing Vehicles with all the pumps behind them, going into the city."

"... you used to volunteer for 'regional calls' (this was a self-help system where fire fighting teams were sent to support other areas) ... we went to London, Bath, Norwich, Bedford, Luton ... you used to take your own vehicle (pump towing vehicle and pump) and your own rations ... they dragged in a pump here and a pump there, into the different places ... I've been through London ... places were blazing away and people crawled out ... it was terrifying ... right down to the docks we used to go."

" ... the overalls ... are what we used to have when we were first formed in the A.F.S. ... we used to have this brown tunic ... a brown smock and brown trousers ... We used to call ourselves the 'brownie boys'...."

"The war hadn't been on long before a full-time Officer (was appointed) who came from London, from Barking, he was an engineer there .... he was good, he did a lot of training for us and he brought the London knowledge to us country bumpkins."

"The fire brigade used to do their rescue work from it (the training structure at Broomin Green) ... We used to do a lot of dummy work down there ..... and those dummies used to weigh on 8 stone, and that wants a bit of picking up and handling up 40 ft, you know .... We used to do hook ladder and rope work."

"We were the parent station to Benington, Walkern and Aston, and we could call those in, or we would go out to them; we were never short of appliances."

"When the warning went you was expected to attend (at the Fire Station) .... You didn't know what to expect, that was part of your duty."

"Then started drifting in full-time men, and they used to man the station, perhaps two on at a time ..... (they) used to man the watch room during the day; it was still manned by volunteers at night-time."

"At night-time, drill night or those nights when it was your rota to go on ... if it was for more than a four hour stretch, you were allowed a little sustenance. You were given some beef roll or something .... one chap used to work at a greenhouse, and we used to supplement it with a tomato or something."

"At the onset of the war, we were as I say, paid for the time we were supposed to have lost at work, and I have answered as many as nine siren calls in a day ..... (on one occasion) I was at work the other side (of Stevenage) at Rooks Nest, Howards End, and the siren goes; well, of course, you come straight down (to the Fire Station) you stand about .... all it is, you are on 'Imminent' (a standby warning meaning raiders are imminent) ... time you got down here (you'd had to put your ladders away, or whatever work you was working on), the all-clear went, so back you go. Well perhaps the warning was on, we'll say 5 to 10 minutes .... (on pay night) the Captain said 'I got your money', he said so many siren calls, so many minutes; and I think I had some paltry sum to come, after attending all those calls ...... out of about nine siren calls I got about half an hour's work, and you got about a shilling an hour, or something."

"....... volunteers used to man the switchboard and were responsible for (warning) the whole of the Civil Defence (Services) around here for miles. Everyone who was within earshot of the siren were dependant on that for a warning that raiders were about, and that was controlled by that room in the fire station."

"We used to be the champions round here for miles, for the whole of the Eastern Counties (fire drill competitions). The team was Charlie Briars, Wally Palmer, Fred Halling and Alby Hunt. We won the Divisional Final, then we went into the Area Finals (No. 12 area), and then from there the winners and runners-up went into the Regional Finals .... we were finalists three times in that."

EVACUEES

"On the first day, 800 evacuees came into Stevenage, and on the second day another 800, and on the third day the same, and so on until they were all in. We took them up to the E.S.A. canteen where they were given, if I remember rightly, a tin of cornbeef, a slab of chocolate and half a pound of biscuits. They were also examined medically. The Government provided all the food."

"I well remember them all coming out of the station ..... there were streams of children all down the hill ...... and the poor W.V.S. trying to get them sorted out."

"We were taken by coach from Stoke Newington, St. Mary's School, to Wood Green and there we were all put on this train .... I can remember somebody saying there is this place called Stevenage up the line and they will take X number of people ..... we were taken off at Stevenage Railway Station and taken to the Town Hall .... and there given little packs of food and drinks; that's when we first arrived ...... Out of the group that I was originally with (I think we must have somehow got parted and herded on these coaches at Wood Green), actually there were very few children that I knew when we finally arrived at Stevenage so I don't know where the others went ... there were lots of women who had been delegated to have X number of children, and my sister and I were taken to Graveley ... when we got there the person wasn't in and we were taken to a Mrs. Cox of the Old Rectory ... and we stayed there ... I was finally evacuated to Mr. Thody ... who used to keep the cobblers shop in Basils Road ... He was very good to me."

'... 1939, we were on holiday and we had to come back ... a Council man knocked on the door and asked how many rooms you had got empty. We said a couple of rooms; in came the mattresses and later in came the 'evacs' (sic) ... First we had children and then their mothers who came and took them back. Then we had families upstairs ... then we had a front room empty and we had a woman and child in there. I think we got eight shillings a week for that .... we had them all the time ..."

"After the official evacuation, we got the private evacuees, mainly mothers with children, and not at all easy to billet."

"We worked in with the Council who were responsible for the evacuation, and they provided us with a room in the Council offices during this period."

"When the mothers etc. visited the children, we had the use of the small Town Hall, and provided tea for them."

"We had one 'little-old-boy', who used to live with us, and you would get up in the morning and would find out he was not there. He had got up before we got up and gone down to Harry James farm to see the cows. He was mad on cows ... he had never seen one. He used to go down there the whole of the day."

"These people came and knocked at the door one night ...... this woman, and she said could we take them in for the night, so I said 'Oh I am sorry, we are full up'. 'My husband' she said, 'is all to pieces'. They came from London. Well, I looked out and I thought, Oh dear, I can't turn them away, he looks terrible, so we brought them in and they stayed for quite a long time ... but he was an ill man. The bombing in London had got him down ... eventually they went back ... Then we had an airman ... he came and asked if we could take them in ... his wife and baby. So we took them in."

" ... if the Cromwell was crowded ... my husband, who as a Special Constable at that time, used to say we have got a spare room, and they used to come and spend the night ... they were only too pleased to come from London and spend the night as long as they got a good night, that was the main thing."

"We did have two people who evacuated themselves and who lived with us for quite a while ... he joined the Report and Control Centre as a volunteer."

"One of the tasks given to the W.V.S. was when we had people coming in from London, people who had been 'bombed-out' and just arrived without warning, we used to take them to the Old Parish Room in Basils Road, and give them tea and make arrangements for them."

"We also took over the St. John's Ambulance hut in Stanmore Road as a clothing exhange; not just for evacuees but for everybody. Later, we transferred it back to the office."

"I did help with an evacuee Brownie Pack ... they had probably been Brownies in London ... Mrs. Kingsland ran the pack ... they used to love getting on the stage at the Parish Rooms and singing or doing little stunts ... and one child never did anything but sing 'I don't want to set the world on fire'."

RESCUE SQUAD

"My department, I was in the rescue Squad, was run by ... who at that time was General Foreman on the Council ... it consisted of nearly all chaps from the building trade ... it was made up into three squads and we was on call for eight hours (or it might have been two squads on call for twelve hours) ... round about a dozen in the squad which included St. John's Ambulance men ... there had to be a leader of each squad ... we used to meet every Tuesday night for training, which used to consist of drinking cups of tea and telling tales ... they had an old army lorry what we used to run about in, and we used to go exercising ... on a place they built for the Fire Brigade down Brum (sic) Green, to do their rescue work."

HOME GUARD

"The first start off, we had wall-bars (batons of circular section timber, cut from lengths of wood intended for use as wall bars in gymnasiums) from the E.S.A... we had to use them before we was issued with rifles ... when the rifles came, they were issued to senior ones first, and the others still had to carry on with wall-bars."

"After Dunkirk, we had to have a barricade in the middle of the road, just outside our place (by south-end Post Office) ..... I was just going to bed one night and I suddenly heard an awful clash of arms and 'Halt, who goes there' and then another voice 'Me you fool'..."

"On one occasion one of our sentries shot a car, which failed to stop in reply to a challenge, and burst a tyre. We then discovered that the car was being driven by one of our Home Guard Officers."

"... up the Avenue ... on the big bit of grass near there the old school used to be, we had a shed up there for gas (training) ... had to take these blokes in with the masks on and give 'em a taste of it ... take them in one at a time, and then get them out ... that was my flipping job."

"When the siren used to go, he used to come tearing home from E.S.A. to get his rifle ... I know I was down the street one day when the siren went, and went tearing home to get the door undone for him to get his gun, and there was army all parked up the side of the road, and they all shouted, 'Go on girl'."

"We had to patrol ... at Knebworth ... you used to have to walk up and down that blooming old coal yard, right up and back again, through Knebworth Station ... I remember Mr. ... another officer, he came up and bawled me one day, down at Knebworth; and I said look 'ere, I says, I've done a days work, I've come 'ere voluntarily, I says, on work for the Home Guard. I says, I go home, I have half hour to wash myself, change and start work again. I says, that's alright for you, you been sleeping all night, while we been on guard."

"We used to go down to the H.Q. at the Stevenage Motor Company, about every third or fourth night for all night guard duty. There was about six of us from our lot. We had to stay on guard all night. We used to go down about 9 o'clock and finish at 6 o'clock in the morning. Then I would come home, have me breakfast and then go straight to work."

"I was transferred to Mr. Bulleid's (Platoon) in the Hitchin Road, and that was where we used to meet ... it was like a private house, and it had a shooting range out the back for 0.22 rifles out in the orchard ..... we used to meet there two or three times a week ... Weekends we used to have manoeuvres, shooting practice, night patrols ... we used to do duty out at St. Pauls Walden Bury."

"I remember one Sunday morning we were out doing a stunt .... the bridge over the line were the station used to be; we had to fill that with barbed wire. Well, of course, troops would have been supplied with proper leather gloves; and we had got no leather gloves; we had to spread that out with our bare hands."

"Another fellow used to take us down to Wymondley pits on the bombs (training); putting the Molotov bombs and the Sticky bombs onto a tank and things like that ... They had been sandpits down there which we used as a firing range ... I remember when the Sten gun first came out (it was only a rough old thing), and we were firing at these targets ... we had to fire so many single shots, and then rapid shots. Well, they gave us the order to fire single shots at the target, and one bloke had his Sten gun on rapid trigger; 'Wooff' ... it nearly frightened him to death."

"We had a 0.22 rifle range in one of the old buildings in the Gas Works in Sish Lane, which was used by all Stevenage Home Guard, and there was also a 0.303 range at Wymondley."

"I remember being on guard one night outside the E.S.A. ... there was a drain (cover) outside the E.S.A. front gate there, and you used to stamp on it ... and that used to give them (the guard inside) a warning if anything was about, so they was always prepard ... that was the code we had between us ... If anybody came down station hill, or anywhere, you used to say 'Halt' ... and stamp on the drain in case there was few more behind ... This bloke came over the station hill about one o'clock (a.m.) ... and I said 'Halt', who goes there'. He said, 'Don't you know who the B... H... I am'. I said, 'No Sir, you could be a German spy, you could be anything'. He said 'I am Mr. Appleton' ... so I stamped on the drain ... and the Sergeant called 'Who is it guard', and I said 'He calls himself Mr. Appleton'. So the Sergeant came out ... and 'Oh' he said, 'Mr. Appleton show me your identification card' ... and we marched him inside; and when we got inside, Mr. Appleton said, 'You B... you wouldn't let me in' ... anyway, he called us all in the office and gave us a scotch each, saying this would keep us warm."

Note: Mr. Appleton was Managing Director of E.S.A.

"Occasionally they (the Home Guard) would have exercises, and we used to cook their meals for them ... we did not do it a lot, only three or four times. They once had a camp at New Wood, Knebworth; a weekend camp and we went and cooked their meals ... they gave us some uniforms ... just to wear for the weekend ... they had an entertainment on the Saturday evening, and we were treated as guests-of-honour ... We got up early next morning and cooked sausages and made porridge out in the open."

One member of the Home Guard when asked if it were ever necessary to use their emergency Headquarters in the 'Coach and Horses' said, "Oh yes boy, every night we had to transfer over there to play dominoes."

"I got in touch with their lot (the 91st Bomb Group of the U.S. 8th Air Force stationed at Bassingbourn) and got permission to take the platoon over there (to Bassingbourn) one Sunday ... we was there all afternoon ... they took us up in their Fortresses and showed us all round ... they made a rare fuss of us ... at teatime ... they gave us sandwiches with grated carrot and cabbage ... they went down well."

PROPAGANDA

"I remember one farmer (who was a real stirrer), who used to come into one of our locals at about 9 o'clock, sit down among the old folk, light his pipe and say 'Well, do you think we are going to win, 'cos I don't, never did'. Or he would say 'I have just been listening to old Haw Haw, he has really got something that chap'. I reckon he would have been lynched in London."

AIR RAID SHELTERS

'... I made up one ... I just built it up. I dug 6 ft underground and built it up with corrugated tin, and then we had beds in there ... My old dog, he'd let us know within 3 or 4 minutes of an air raid ... he used to yap to get out the door, and as soon as I let him out the door, he used to jump straight over the little fence and straight up the garden path and he was up the shelter before we got there."

AIR RAIDS

"We had a land-mine dropped which broke a lot of windows in the High Street. It fell during the night near

Broomin Green Farm. It even shattered some glass windows in Hellards Road and a house in Brick Kiln, Lane which was badly damaged, was shorn up for a long time."

"I remember that land-mine dropping over by Broomin Green. I was up the E.S.A. at the time .... I was in the A.R.P. and they had the old dug-outs there ... we were just coming up out of the dug-out, to go round the works, when that (the mine) went off. Well, you know where that is (Broomin Green), it's about a mile way, and if you had been up there and heard all the mud and stones falling on the sheds ..."

"I used to have my (sewing) machine in the front room bay .... I was machining one day and the kids were coming up the path from school .. and over the top of the tree .. there was a 'plane, and I looked and I stared at this 'ere pilot, and I thought now whatever has got a thing (marking) like that ... it was a blooming Jerry."

"I saw that one (enemy aircraft) that day what dropped that bomb in the factory ... that was following the railway that was ... it wasn't very high above the railway ... I was in the old Council Yard ... 'Cos he never got away."

"When that 'doodle-bug' came down, he (her husband) had got them both (their children) under the stairs ... and he said, 'Now be quiet, 'cos there might be a big bang in a minute' .... and 'cos it sailed over, and ended up in a field near Luton ... (one of the children said), 'We never heard a bang', and they were disappointed 'cos there was no bang ... That only just cleared Stevenage ... if that had been another 20 yards that way, that would not have cleared that (E.S.A.) chimney ... it was only just above the chimney pots ... and was it going! ... it was vibrating the things on the mantelpiece."

"When the 'doodle-bugs' started falling ... and the shells ... I went over Norton Green and picked a lot of stuff up, and they used to have a box outside Shelford and Crowe ... for scrap."

FACTORY WORKERS

"I was already in the E.S.A. Fire Brigade, and then when war broke out, we went over to A.R.P. for the factory ... When war first started, we used to have to get up and go up there every time the siren went, and that used to go about 3 or 4 times a day. Soon as you got home and got back into bed, you had to get up, and go back up there again. Well, they stopped that, and they made a rota so that you spent a whole night up there. About every 4th night I think it was."

"When we was up the E.S.A. we used to collect for all the troops ... all the blokes who were serving who were E.S.A. ... they used to ask you first, how much you would like stopped out your wages ... for the comfort funds they used to call it."

"I was on the Mosquito aircraft ... in the Dope Shop ... the wing started in the jigs ... the men worked on it, and then it came on the 'floor' and they did all the bonding electrical things ... and then they put the bits on the ends of the wings ... they were covered in screw holes and we had to 'stop' all those up with 'stopper', and when it was dry, rub it all down ... all the edges and seams had to be 'doped'. We had to paint the dope on by hand."

"Well first of all they (Mosquito aircraft), were a Reconnaissance plane .... and they made them into a bomber. I used to do the big tank doors underneath the wing, and then when they made them into bombers, I used to do the bomb rack in the centre of the wing."

"I was working down at the Knitting Company (Sish Lane), when war first started ..... the Gas Company and the gas holders were just behind, and when the warning used to go in the day, we used to come out and go home .... he (the boss) would not let us stay there, he thought it was too dangerous, and we used to go home until it was all over."

TROOP CONVOYS

" ... Army convoys coming through the town ... and all the garages served army petrol ... the Service Corps who were with them, used to come and unlock the petrol pumps and serve the petrol ... the petrol was coloured brown."

"I can remember one very very foggy night, there was a hell of a noise outside the shop ... and we opened the shop door to find a tank just coming past the shop door ... he had mounted up the path between the trees and the shop ... it was so foggy he thought that was the path to follow."

"I remember Doctor Margaret Swayne having all the women, one Sunday afternoon ... at the Astonia Cinema ..... and gave us all a 'pep' talk on all the vices ... so that we wouldn't get into trouble with all the soldiers."

OLD CASTLE CANTEEN

"We used to do a tremendous trade; you see, the soldiers were coming through ... we didn't put them up for the night, they used to be billeted in Witney Wood ... we used to cook their food for them ... the biggest number we had was 1200 one night ... There was an upstairs as well, which we always said was haunted ... we used to hear old Trigg walk across the floor sometimes ... mostly things with chips ... eggs, cheese, baked beans, sandwiches ... they didn't pay very much, just a small charge ... it was all good fun really."

"I used to do three nights a week down there ... we used to get a lot of the American forces in there ... they used to come from Steeple Morden ... there was one chap ... and he came in one night, and had plenty of drink, and he wanted coffee. Well, we were very very busy ... eventually I gave him the coffee. Well, you know how little we had, and he said 'You call this God-damn stuff coffee; ... I'd had a very hard day ... and was very very tired, so I just sat down and really tore him off a strip, and told him that we didn't have any coffee, and he was jolly lucky to get it ... in the end he burst into tears. And after that, he must have put the word around, because every time they came in they used to bring us chocolate and things like that."

"I remember Bassingbourn very well ... one of the (U.S) officers came in one night, and said to Helen Inns, because she was the organiser ... they wanted some nice young ladies to go to a forces dance, you see, and he asked her to come along as well, presumably as chaperon ... it was really so funny because they sent this covered waggon for us, and we were in there with all the blinds drawn down, we were not supposed to know where we were going, it was all very secret, and they drove us right into the place before they let us out ... they had turned a mess or something into a cloakroom for us ladies, and in there was a notice - TO ALL BASSINGBOURN PERSONNEL."

LIST OF ABBREVIATIONS

A.F.S.	Auxiliary Fire Service
A.F.V.	Armoured Fighting Vehicle
A.R.P.	Air Raid Precautions
A.R.W.	Air Raid Warning
A/T	Anti-Tank
A.T.C.	Air Training Corps
A.T.S.	Auxiliary Territorial Service
B.B.C.	British Broadcasting Corporation
C.D.	Civil Defence
D.L.	Defended Locality
'Fly'	Flying Bomb (V.1)
G.T.C.	Girls' Training Corps
H.C.C.	Hertfordshire County Council
H.E.	High Explosive
H.Q.	Headquarters
I.B.	Incendiary Bomb
L.A.	Light Automatic
L.C.C.	London County Council
L.D.V.	Local Defence Volunteers
L.M.G.	Light Machine Gun
L.R.R.	Long Range Rocket (V.2)
N.F.S.	National Fire Service
R.A.F.	Royal Air Force
R.P.G.	Rounds Per Gun
S.F.P.	Supplementary Fire Party
S.I.P.	Self-Igniting Phosphorus
Sch. Log.	Letchmore Road School Log-Book entry
T.S.M.G.	Thompson Sub-Machine Gun
U.X.B.	Unexploded Bomb
V.E.	Victory Europe
V.J.	Victory Japan
W.A.A.F.	Women's Auxiliary Air Force
W.V.S.	Women's Voluntary Services for Civil Defence

BIBLIOGRAPHY

Allingham	M.	THE OAKEN HEART	1941
Beauman	K.	GREEN SLEEVES: The Story of The W.V.S.	1977
Birtles	P.	THE MOSQUITO	1980
Blackson	G.	A HISTORY OF THE BRITISH FIRE SERVICE	1957
Briggs	S.	KEEP SMILING THROUGH	1975
Brown	R.	EAST ANGLIA 1939	1980
Collier	B.	THE DEFENCE OF THE UNITED KINGDOM	1957
Craufurd	R.	COUNTRY WOMEN AT WAR	-
Demarne	C.	THE LONDON BLITZ: A Fireman's Tale	1980
Fleming	P.	INVASION 1940	1957
Glover	G.	CIVIL DEFENCE	1938
Grant	I.	THE COUNTRYSIDE AT WAR	1975
Graves	C.	THE HOME GUARD OF BRITAIN	1943
Graves	C.	WOMEN IN GREEN: The Story of the W.V.S.	1948
Haldane	J.B.S.	A.R.P.	1938
Harrison	T.	LIVING THROUGH THE BLITZ	1976
H.M.S.O.		NATIONAL SERVICE	1939
Johnson	D.	EAST ANGLIA AT WAR, 1939-45	1978
Lampe	D.	THE LAST DITCH	1968
Lindsay	G.	THE WAR ON THE CIVIL AND MILITARY FRONTS	1942
Longmate	N.	HOW WE LIVED THEN	1971
Longmate	N.	THE REAL DAD'S ARMY	1974

MacNalty	A.	MEDICAL SERVICES IN WAR	1968
Marwick	A.	THE HOME FRONT	1976
Minns	R.	BOMBERS & MASH: The Domestic Front 1939-45	1980
Newman	M.	HOW STEVENAGE HELPED PUT A SPITFIRE IN THE SKY Hertfordshire Countryside, October 1980	
Nixon	B.	RAIDERS OVERHEAD: A Diary of the London Blitz	1980
O'Brien	T.	CIVIL DEFENCE	1955
Sackville West	V.	THE WOMEN'S LAND ARMY	1944
Titmus	R.	PROBLEMS OF SOCIAL POLICY	1950
Wittering	W.	STEVENAGE GOES TO WAR Hertfordshire Countryside, July 1978	
White	D.	D FOR DORIS, V FOR VICTORY	1981
Yass	M.	THE HOME FRONT, ENGLAND 1939-45	1971